WHAT TO EAT NOW

Dedicated to my mother and father, who taught me to approach life like one would the fridge. Get in there, have a thorough rootle around, take what you like without making a mess, and then make something good.

And my brother and sister, for being creamy.

Val Weaver

WHAT TO EAT NOW

THE BEST OF AUTUMN AND WINTER EATING

VALENTINE WARNER

PHOTOGRAPHS BY HOWARD SOOLEY

MITCHELL BEAZLEY

What to Eat Now
by Valentine Warner

First published in Great Britain in 2008 by Mitchell Beazley,
an imprint of Octopus Publishing Group Limited,
2–4 Heron Quays, London E14 4JP.
www.octopusbooks.co.uk

An Hachette Livre UK Company
www.hachettelivre.co.uk

ISBN: 978 1 84533 450 5

A CIP record for this book is available from the British Library

Set in Gotham-Book

Colour reproduction by AltaImage UK
Printed and bound in Italy by Amilcare Pizzi

Commissioning Editor Becca Spry
Art Director Tim Foster
Design and Art Direction Caz Hildebrand
Editorial Director Tracey Smith
Project Editor Leanne Bryan
Photographer Howard Sooley
Production Manager Peter Hunt
Editor Susan Fleming
Proofreaders Hattie Ellis and Jo Richardson
Home Economists Steve Parle and Justine Pattison
Styling Isabel de Cordova
Recipe Testers Trish Davies, Joanna Farrow and Justine Pattison
Indexer Diana Lecore

Based on the BBC TWO TV series *What to Eat Now*
produced by Optomen Television Ltd

BBC optomen

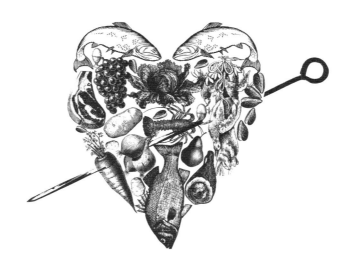

CONTENTS

AN INTRODUCTION

'Not another cookbook!' you cry. Well, this one is about autumn and some of its champions, with recipes to sustain us on into winter's mean months. It starts when the swallow's shadow flickers over the waters, away from the din of absurd contraptions that blow leaves from A to B.

In these pages is an assortment of modest dishes for the frugal, with big hitters for those who might relish wiping their shiny chins. There are recipes for those in a hurry and others for those moving at a more leisurely pace. Find soups to warm the extremities when frozen hands feel they might smash like china, and slow-cooked succulence for returning walkers moving towards the pumpkin glow of home at dusk. Overall, this is a book to accompany the browns, oranges and yellows of falling leaves – the first frosts, bigger coats and log fires – and to encourage joyful activity instead of 4pm gloom.

This is my first book, so if you seek assurance through famous chefs, then I cannot smoke your haddock, and you should return it to the display. What I do know is that in my loving marriage to the pot, I have witnessed a few knives licked clean and plates tilted to the swipe of bread and finger. So if you are still inquisitive, take this book home with you or ask if you can borrow it. (Although personally I never lend books, records or fishing tackle.)

Autumn is the most fecund time, leaving winter looking meaner in its menu and requiring a little more imagination beside the stove. But throughout both seasons there is plenty to store away, fatten us up and celebrate with knife and fork. Picture pheasants hopping into fruiting hedgerows, competing giant marrows on straining trestles, mushrooms popping up in the rusty bracken, clouds of mackerel shoaling off the beaches, oysters fat in their houses, roots galore and cheeses which, like lamb, are the product of rich, grass-fed summers. Think of apples thumping on to the dewy ground, tender lettuces, skeins of geese settling on the salt flats, partridges hunkered down in the plough furrows and mussels sweet, plump and revitalized from spring loving. Buttered sprouts, fat hams, and sweet parsnips, these are but a hint of the goodies to set upon a table groaning under the weight of options and I am sorry to say that I have, no doubt, left some out. This is because I have concentrated, in the main, on the more regular visitors to my tiny flat.

Seasonal cooking allows life to become simple; in effect, the opposite of a world market and the fashion for the far-flung so eloquently coined by

Hugh Fearnley-Whittingstall as the 'idolization of the exotic'. Cooking by seasons makes it clear what I have to work with. It encourages inventiveness and reintroduces the forgotten or ignored. It simmers, sizzles and steams in harmony with nature's rhythms, so important in an age when we seem so removed from them, using the choicest ingredients far fresher than insipid imitations hurried along under a distant sun.

I would be a liar if I suggested that I never reach for the occasional orange, dried pulse, chilli, date or spice, but all the following recipes – even those brought back from abroad – fundamentally rely on things found in our waters, fields and woods. The great and quietly spoken chef, Fergus Henderson, is often known to remark, 'What a treat', and so far as seasonal food is concerned, for me that is the point. Things become a treat because you have to wait for them, and when they do come along, you are pretty sure they will be delicious because *this is rightfully their time*. And the timing is impeccable, as by no happy chance their arrival coincides with the necessity to eat heartily throughout the next four months, bolstering our minds and bodies through the increasing cold, grizzling discontent and dark.

This does not mean to say you are reading a gourmand's manual to instant gout, but neither is this a slimmer's guide. It is not gratuitous in its use of butter or duck fat, but not shy either, so if your appetite leans towards egg-white omelettes and year-round rocket salads, I doubt you will revel in much of the following.

Who knows what climate change will bring, but right now I can hear Mother Nature singing in the kitchen on this January evening. It is cold and in roughly an hour I will be eating venison stew and cabbage; mangetout and tomatoes could not be further from my mind.

A FEW MORE THINGS

For many of us, the kitchen is a cherished room in which the outdoors is brought indoors and transformed into something wonderful. Food can only taste as good as the love invested in it. If good ingredients have been nurtured with care, then from the minute you take them home, like a relay runner, you have been passed the baton to continue that care.

Cook only what you have time to cook well. If you are distracted or in a hurry things will almost certainly suffer. But don't be put off by recipes that have long cooking times. Providing you have a good internal brain timer, or an orange plastic one, these recipes will allow you to go off and do other things. Slow cooking was invented for this reason. Overall, the recipes in this book are simple, and regardless of the time they take to cook, their preparation is easy.

If I have noticed one thing about how people use cookbooks, it is that they can be impatient. Methods should be followed carefully; if it says a pan should be smoking hot, a pear peeled or the water should simmer gently, it is important that you do that.

To the eye what you are cooking might appear good, but that is not enough to go on, so check, prod, mess up, rectify or start again. Above all, taste everything as you go.

Shopping and foraging: When choosing ingredients, decide carefully and ask questions, as a great deal is to be learnt from those that know and will give you their time.

When out in the field, it is so easy to be in a rush. How many times have I forgotten to pick the wild garlic by my sister's house before returning to London, or failed to ask what breed of beef I have just bought, or driven straight past a little fishing town, fiddling with the CD player, when I should have been seeing if the boats are in? Too many!

Binning: An excellent chef I worked under, when seeing pans heading towards the sink, would always look up from his cooking. 'What's wrong with that?', he would say pointing with a spatula. I would frown into the empty pot replying, 'What?'. 'That,' he would say again, now standing next to me and pointing directly at a tiny splash of sauce left in the bottom of the pot. 'Is that particular bit not nice?'. Good point! If you have made something and loved it, don't waste it.

Know what's in your fridge: In moments of carelessness, I feel very sad at having to bin that tiny, forgotten slice of terrine left behind the new sparkly things I chose instead, when the fridge light shined on them. It will also help you to be inventive when having meals comprised of leftovers – possibly the birth of fresh catastrophe, but hopefully frugal brilliance or at least sustenance.

Leftovers: Here and there, underneath certain recipes, you will find suggestions for the afterlife, ways to reinvent leftovers. Concerning trimmings from leeks mushrooms and the like, although your kitchen does not operate like a restaurant, they can be good additions to stock, and stale bread is for breadcrumbs etcetera, etcetera. Unfortunately, I do not have an allotment, chickens or a pig, or even a garden.

So far I have not discovered a truly responsible way of getting rid of cooking oil. I'm beginning to get the impression that the arteries of London's sewerage system increasingly resemble those of someone straining under a diet of crispy twizzlers and burgers, with vast spadefuls of clogged fat cut away from the damp brickwork and carted off in barrows. Pretty Dickensian. I would suggest letting it cool and either straining it for re-use or decanting it into a bottle and sending it off in the correct rubbish.

Kit: When buying basic equipment, I recommend buying things that last. Life is too short for bad kit, the aromas of the food hidden by that of a melting pan handle. Using good equipment will make the cooking, as well as the eating, more enjoyable.

That's about it, although I always forget something, like the trail of clothes I leave in people's houses.

ENTER MEAT!

Val Warner

FOUR LEGS

LAMB

Lamb eaten in autumn, born in March and grazed on summer's grasses, is far more flavoursome than the Easter table lambs that require endless processed feed, warmth and husbandry through the mean months – hence the price.

For me, the cut to make a beeline for is the shoulder. A little fattier and harder to carve than a leg it may be, but cooked well it can be deliciously tender, pale and sweet. The shoulder responds well to a long, slow cook or briefer treatments over hot embers.

In fact, any part of the top end of a lamb, such as the breast or neck, is very versatile, keeping me awake late in semi-conscious cooking delirium, thinking of ideas when I should be counting sheep.

There are many skilled sheep breeders all over the UK, and I am drawn more towards meat that has wandered the hills and mountains or salty shores, nibbling on the hedges and herbs, picking and choosing as they wish. With so much good lamb at home, pop the other stuff in a jiffy bag addressed 'New Zealand – Return to Sender'.

LAMB BIRRIA (Mexican Lamb Stew)

In parts of Mexico it can get very cold. The backbone to Lamb Birria is a combination of dried chillies, which produces a fabulous slow burn that will creep out to your extremities, warming them with a very pleasant heat. Although many varieties of dried chilli are available in a few supermarkets and specialist shops in the UK, obtaining them still involves a certain amount of tapping about on the internet. Proper Mexican food is only just beginning to flash its gold tooth in this country, so do not confuse muddled Tex-Mex stodge with the incredible dishes you will find from Tijuana to Yucatán.

For availability, replace the Mexican ancho or pasilla chilli with the Spanish choricero. Guanjillo and guajillo chillies are the same. I have added bird's eye chillies to ramp up the heat in the absence of the ancho chilli.

Serves 4-6

2kg lamb's neck, leg or shoulder meat, off the bone
4 bird's eye chillies
flour and water paste, for sealing the pot
1 small onion, peeled

MARINADE
6 dried guajillo or guanjillo chillies
6 dried pasilla or ancho chillies

1 large onion, peeled and coarsely chopped
7 good hard garlic cloves, peeled
125ml cider vinegar
1 level tablespoon large-flaked sea salt
1 level teaspoon cumin seeds
3 whole cloves
1 level tablespoon dried oregano
10 black peppercorns
10 bay leaves

Cut the meat into fat chunks. It needs to sit in its chilli marinade for 12 hours in the fridge before use to ensure the flavours penetrate the meat.

Remove the stalk, seeds and membrane from the guanjillo and choricero chillies. Rip them up into 50-pence-sized pieces (although these chillies are not violently hot, it may be worth using rubber gloves). Put a frying pan on a low heat and throw in the chilli pieces. It is essential that you do not burn the chillies, as they will become bitter. They should be kept moving while toasting to ensure all the pieces get a bit of the action. This does require all your attention. You will notice the chillies begin to take on a paler tobacco colour. If you feel nervous, just stop this process a little earlier than one normally would. You should, however, still smell a wonderful, rich, sweet, nutty, woody aroma. Turn off the heat and pour some hot water from the kettle over the chillies to cover them, and leave them to hydrate for at least half an hour.

When done, put the onion, garlic, vinegar, salt, cumin, cloves, oregano and chillies with their water into a blender and blitz to a smooth paste. Pass this into a large bowl through a sieve, pressing down with the back of a spoon to leave a rich, deep red, tangy, loose purée. Discard what's left in the sieve, ensuring no purée is thrown away. Add the peppercorns, bay and chunks of meat. Mix together thoroughly, cover and leave in the fridge overnight.

On the day of use, preheat the oven to 170°C/325°F/Gas 3.

Put all the lamb into a heavy lidded casserole or earthenware pot. Crumble in the bird's eye chillies and mix through. (Definitely wear your rubber gloves, as these are very hot.) Put the lid on the pot and seal the edges all the way round with a rudimentary flour and water paste. This will turn the pot into more of a pressure cooker and produce very tender meat. Cook in the preheated oven for 3 hours. While the meat cooks, chop the small onion into neat, fine dice, then rinse under a cold tap to mellow. Drain the onion well.

When the hour comes, crack off the seal carefully to avoid any crust falling into the stew. Take the dish to the table and serve the stew in deep bowls sprinkled with the chopped onion and a little extra dried oregano. Eat this stew with warm tortillas and bottles of chilled beer or bitter. *Suerte*!

NOTE: *Speciality chillies are available from a variety of sources including Brindisa (www.brindisa.com; 02074 071036) and The Cool Chile Company (www.coolchile.co.uk; 0870 9021145).*

LAMB'S KIDNEYS WITH SHERRY AND SMOKED PAPRIKA

Uncomplicated and robust, this smoky-tasting dish cheers the soul when alone, and is a good breakfast start to any cold day, when you can see your breath upon stepping outside. I shall write it for two.

Serves 2

4 lamb's kidneys, rinsed and patted dry
1 large onion
1 tablespoon olive oil
25g butter
large-flaked sea salt and black pepper

2 tablespoons Amontillado sherry
   (any will do)
a splash of red wine vinegar
$1/2$ teaspoon *pimentón de la Vera* (hot
   smoked paprika)
2 slices of bread, toasted and buttered

Have the kidneys cleaned of their skins by your butcher. Slice the kidneys in half lengthways, then with a small, sharp knife, cut out the undesirable white middle of each piece.

Peel the onion and cut it in half, top to bottom. Lie it on its flat side and cut it into the thinnest slivers you are capable of. When cut and cooked like this, they really wrap around the kidney, as opposed to diced onions, which fall off as they approach your mouth.

Heat the oil with the butter and give the onions a head start, frying them on a medium heat until they are really soft and beginning to colour. Turn up the heat a little and add the kidney pieces, making sure they are touching the pan, not just sitting on top of the onions. Fry them for 3 minutes, letting them be still in order to catch and colour. Season the onions and kidneys with salt and pepper. The onions want to caramelize, too, but if they are burning, manoeuvre them around the kidneys. Turn the kidneys and fry on the other side for another 2 minutes. Add the sherry, vinegar and pimentón and stir for 30 seconds while the contents sizzle and spit.

Sit on buttered toast and pour over the sweet juices. Keen on a morning steadier, I will sometimes accompany the kidneys with a tiny glass of the sherry.

ROAST SHOULDER OF LAMB WITH BITTER HERBS AND HONEY

In late September on a blisteringly hot Greek day, I stopped my walk to drink the last of my warm water. The afternoon heat had released an overwhelming smell of camomile, sage and wild thyme on the mountain, which, coupled with the deafening racket of the cicadas, made for a heady experience. Nearby a large flock of scrawny sheep arrived, nibbling their way uphill, their tinny bells clinking away. As they barged on through the dry bushes, it struck me that these bitter mountain herbs and sheep could make a good, long, slow-cooked dish. I pulled up what herbs I needed and the next day went to the butcher with plans. I think it works well.

Serves 4

1 x 1.4kg shoulder of lamb (get your butcher to split the protruding forearm)
1 proper handful of loose dried camomile (or rip open 4 camomile teabags)
1/2 bunch of fresh thyme, leaves picked
4 sprigs of fresh rosemary, leaves picked
12 fresh sage leaves, roughly chopped
1 tablespoon dried oregano
large-flaked salt and black pepper
juice of 1 lemon
about 1 tablespoon good Greek or wild flower runny honey
2 tablespoons olive oil
125ml water

Preheat the oven to 200°C/400°F/Gas 6.

Take the shoulder of lamb and, with the tip of a sharp knife, make shallow scores through the outer layer of skin and fat, but not into the meat, cross-hatching the entire surface. Do this on both sides. In a bowl, combine your dried camomile with the thyme, rosemary, sage and oregano. Add a heavy grind of black pepper and a good tablespoon of salt. Make sure these are well blended. Take a handful of this mix and press it into the skin of the lamb, massaging it in well on all sides.

Sprinkle some of the herb mix across the bottom of a heavy lidded casserole. Place the lamb on top, and then squeeze the lemon juice across the top before sprinkling with the remaining herb mix. Trail the honey across the top of the shoulder. Pour over a little olive oil as well, then splash 125ml water into the bottom of the pan.

Put the lid on, get it into the preheated oven and cook for 2½ hours. Check after 1 hour: the lamb should be taking on a little colour. If the water has dried out, add a dash more, the idea being that the water keeps the lamb moist while cooking, leaving you with a good, dark, syrupy juice.

The lamb flesh should pull away nicely from the bone, and I suggest that you eat it with the potatoes on page 186, but replacing the duck fat with olive oil.

ROAST SHOULDER OF LAMB AND ROOT VEGETABLES WITH ONION SAUCE

This really is a warming and happy-making lunch. Eat it wrapped in a large woollen jersey for the whole sheep experience.

I'm surprised I was not put off eating this first at school. I never reacted with the same eagerness as my contemporaries when Flying Saucers (deep-fried Spam) or Maryland Chicken were served up, but always smiled to myself as the grey, overcooked lamb appeared, daubed in anaemic onion sauce. No doubt another behavioural oddity that classed me as one of the weirdos. Maybe it's unwise to mention school food when hoping your reader will try a dish, but I assure you this version is excellent.

Serves 4

3 big sprigs of fresh rosemary
large-flaked sea salt and black pepper
1 x 1.4kg shoulder of lamb
4 Jerusalem artichokes, if available
6 medium carrots
6 small parsnips
olive oil

ONION SAUCE
3 medium onions
25g butter
200ml dry white wine
1 heaped teaspoon caster sugar
2 teaspoons white wine vinegar
1 tablespoon plain flour
400ml milk
50ml water

Preheat the oven to 220°C/425°F/Gas 7.

On a board, strip the rosemary from its stems, combining the leaves with 1 tablespoon salt and a heavy bombardment of black pepper. Chop this all together until you are left with a lichen-coloured rosemary-salt mix. Take the lamb shoulder and, with the tip of a sharp knife, lightly score the top side with close parallel lines, making sure you do not cut into the meat. Rub in the salt and rosemary mix, really massaging it into the scoring you have made, and not forgetting the under side of the joint. Leave the lamb to one side.

Peel the Jerusalem artichokes, carrots and parsnips, splitting the parsnips and artichokes in half lengthways. Put them straight into salted boiling water and parboil them all for no more than 6 minutes. Cool immediately under a cold tap in a colander. Toss them in a bowl in a little olive oil, black pepper and salt.

On a baking tray, lay the vegetables in their respective groups, placing the lamb directly on top of them all, scored side up. Lightly pour a little olive oil over the top of the shoulder. Cook it in the preheated oven for approximately 45-55 minutes, turning the vegetables after 30 minutes. The joint should be pink, but not raw. Take a secretive slice from a hidden part of the shoulder. Don't wing it. Taking meat to the table only to remove it for further cooking is a disappointment to all.

Meanwhile, peel and halve the onions, and finely dice each onion half. Melt the butter in a pan, throw in the onion with some salt and a good grind of black pepper and sweat for 10 minutes. Pour in the wine, sprinkle in the sugar and cook until the onion is soft, another 20 minutes, stirring every now and then. Add the vinegar at this point, and keep on cooking until the liquid has evaporated. The onions should not be coloured. Sprinkle over the flour and stir it in thoroughly. Use a whisk, as it is effective for eradicating lumps.

Start adding the milk slowly, in dribs and drabs, stirring all the time. When all the milk has been used, cook the sauce very gently for a further 10 minutes. The consistency of the sauce should be that of running double cream. Season it. The onion sauce is one step away from ready.

Remove the lamb and place it on a board to rest. Cover it loosely with foil to retain the heat. Stick the vegetables back in the oven and cook them for a further 10 minutes before placing them on a platter. Put the oven tray on the hob, and pour in 50ml water, stirring vigorously to lift any 'catchings' and juices. Pour this juice through a sieve into your onion sauce and stir in.

Carve the lamb and lay it over the vegetables, taking the trouble to pour any additional juices leftover from cooking the joint into the sauce. Pour the sauce around the handsome sliced shoulder and roots.

This is one heck of a lunch.

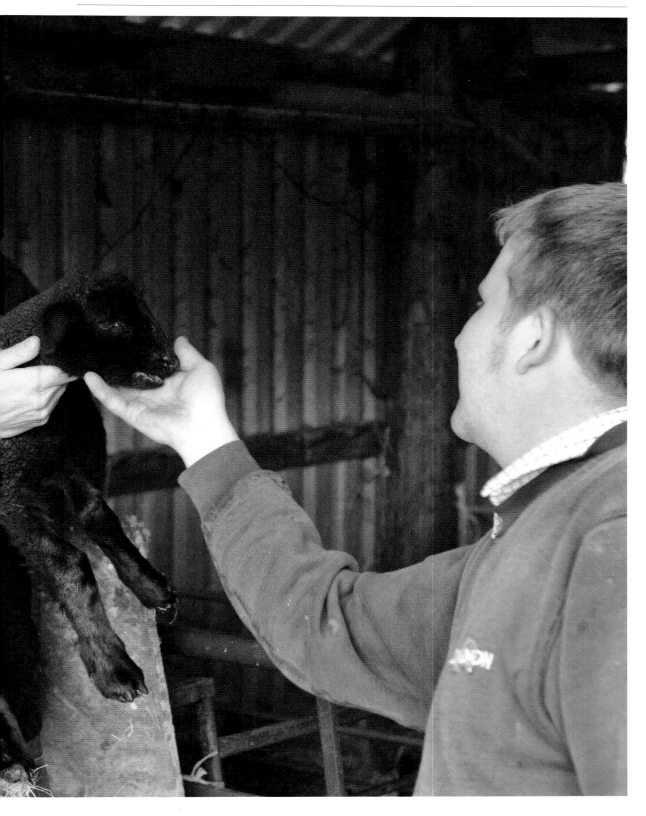

PORK

When Beatrix Potter named one of her heroes 'Pigling Bland' I think she got it slightly wrong. There's nothing bland about piggy – boiled hams and parsley sauce, liver and bacon, plump sausages, steaming faggots, shiny pies and irresistible crisp and fatty rinds to fork from the plates of fussy eaters. No, the pig is a generous beast and one of my favourite animals, whether taken to table or observed from the gate post.

When the clocks go back it is regularly pig o'clock, good days often start with black pudding and eggs, later followed by regular afternoon visits to the fridge for another go at the *jamón*. Evening trips to the pub never seem fully rounded without a packet of scratchings.

Pork tourism will often find me unable to resist street offerings, once pushed too far in Mexico, but that is an unsuitable tale for this book.

We are a nation of pig keepers, with an exceptional tradition of pork accomplishments. So many local recipes at the heart of our cuisine came about to enable cuts and offal to keep longer, into the harsher winter months, rather than spoiling in the warmth of summer. Hence our great tradition of smoking, salting and potting grew, and for such dishes the pigs were slaughtered in the end of autumn.

I would love to communicate in 'piggish', as I feel most breeds would be quite outspoken.

SWEET AND SMOKY BARBECUED PORK WITH ROAST BEETROOT AND COLESLAW

Why does everyone stop lighting barbecues when the weather turns cold? Surely as a nation of bonfire nuts it is as good a time as any to cook outside. If however, it is too cold for you, don a nearby petroleum by-product fur coat and pretend to be early man toasting his closely guarded chunk of sandy flesh. With your face dramatically lit by the flickering glow as you baste, trimming morsels to taste with burnt fingers, time will pass quickly. As you carry the piece of handsome meat into the light, you will feel good and proud that you lit the barbecue when the weather was cold and the day short.

This treatment calls for the meat to cook slowly and those horrid little choking, fuel-soaked, throw-away barbecues will not do. That includes lighting six in succession. Don't worry, I'm including the oven version too.

Serves 6

2kg pork neck, skin removed (get your
    butcher to do this)
24 cloves
1 tablespoon large-flaked sea salt
1 heaped tablespoon muscovado sugar

MARINADE
1 onion, peeled and blended to a pulp
200ml red wine vinegar
2 teaspoons fennel seeds

1 teaspoon dried oregano
2 level tablespoons *pimentón de la Vera*
2 teaspoons flaked or powdered chipolte
2 teaspoons English mustard powder
50ml strong coffee
2 tablespoons black treacle
2 teaspoons black peppercorns, crushed
1 x 140g tin tomato purée

TO SERVE
roast beetroot (*see* page 201)
coleslaw (*see* page 173)

Start this recipe a day before you want to eat it. Combine all the marinade
ingredients with 125ml water and blend thoroughly in the food processor.

Lay the pork on a board and, with the tip of a sharp knife, score
shallow cuts down it, in lines rather like a ploughed field. Score the other way
too, so that it is criss-crossed. Do this on all sides. Stud with the cloves, 12 per
side. Put in a non-metal container, pour over the marinade and make sure it is
covered. Store in the fridge overnight, turning twice.

If using a barbecue, light it and wait until the embers are white with
glimpses of orange showing through. Lay the meat on the grill and have your
carving knife and fork and a board nearby. Have the marinade in a pan on the
edge of the heat. If you have one, put the lid on the barbecue and open the
vents. (The lid ensures a more even, gentler cook, and keeps the coals burning
longer. Without a lid, the meat will take longer to cook and you will need to
turn it more often.) Baste the side to be grilled and turn over with the fork
every 15 minutes. If you are running out of marinade, add a splash of water.

After an hour, sprinkle on one side with half the salt and sugar; don't
be shy. Cook for 5 minutes, then turn over, sprinkle with the remaining salt
and sugar and cook for another 5 minutes. It should now be ready. Remove to
the board and cut into the centre about halfway. The meat should be soft and
wet, leaving you with the sense that the pink has just gone from the centre.

If cooking this in the oven, preheat the oven to 180°F/350°F/Gas 4.
Lay the joint on a rack with a tray underneath and baste with the marinade
before roasting for 20 minutes. Baste it again and cook for a further 20
minutes; while cooking, mix the muscovado sugar and salt in a bowl. Increase
the temperature to 240°C/475°F/Gas 9. Cook for a further 30 minutes then
repeat the basting and sprinkle over half the salt and brown sugar mix. Cook
for a further 5 minutes, until it caramelizes. Turn the joint and sprinkle with
the remaining sugar and salt and cook for the last 5 minutes. Remove the
pork and rest it for 5 minutes. It should be the faintest pink inside. Slice
thickly and serve with the rest of the marinade, simmered for 15 minutes.

Eat with the beetroots and coleslaw.

ROAST SUCKLING PIG FOR NEW YEAR'S EVE

I have tried many variations of piglet, which I will go for at any given opportunity. I have enjoyed most, with the exception of one I ate in north-east India, which I would suggest was, despite its size, actually a pig so old that all the other pigs went to seek advice from it. It was not only inedible but also very hairy for one apparently so young.

Order suckling pig through your butcher in advance, as they often take a while to arrive.

Serves 12-15

1 x 9-10kg piglet
the piglet liver (if available) and kidneys
3 large onions
a large knob of butter
2 large thumb-sized pieces of fresh root
    ginger, finely chopped
a large handful of fresh thyme sprigs

300g black pudding, crumbled
3 medium Bramley apples, peeled, cored
    and roughly chopped
1 large white farmhouse bloomer loaf
a large handful of parsley, finely chopped
large-flaked sea salt and black pepper
vegetable oil
330ml cider, ideally organic

This does require a double oven and, worrying that I may exclude some people who want to cook it, I have included some notes on cooking a smaller piglet at the end of this recipe.

Instruct that the piglet be singed and scraped of hair. Have the butcher score it all the way round with 8cm gaps between each score from neck to rump. He should also make six alternate holes on each side of the belly cavity; they must be big enough to poke the string through with a chopstick.

Peel, halve and finely slice the onions, and sweat them in the butter over a low heat with the finely chopped fresh ginger and stripped thyme. Chop the liver and kidneys. After about 20 minutes, when the onion is soft and pale golden, turn up the heat a little and throw them in with the crumbled black pudding. Fry until the offal and pudding are obviously cooked, about 10 minutes. Turn the contents into a large bowl and add the apples, the bread torn into matchbox-sized chunks and the parsley. Mix everything together thoroughly. Take a bit of this mixture and, fashioning it into a wee patty, fry it in a little extra butter until cooked. Taste it and doctor the stuffing accordingly with salt and pepper until seasoned perfectly.

Preheat the oven to 200°C/400°F/Gas 6.

Turn the piglet upside down and pack the stuffing into the empty cavity. Tie the string through the first hole at the head end and fasten a knot around the hole. Pass the string alternately, criss-crossing the belly through all the holes, drawing the sides together tightly. Secure the opposite end with a knot.

Take a shelf from the oven and line the area where the piggy will sit with doubled-over tin foil, as this will help it release in case it needs moving on to a platter later. Lay the piglet on top, trotters down. You will have to slightly manipulate the stiff legs to get the piglet into a happy sitting position. If this is hard, steady the legs with string tied around each trotter, with the string crossing the rump or back. Make sure that underneath where the shelf sits you place a tray to catch any falling juices. Rub the piglet's skin all over with vegetable oil before applying generous amounts of salt.

Put the piglet in the oven, head towards the door. Baste the entire piglet with some of the fat collected in the tray about once every 45 minutes. After about $2^1/2$ hours, check to see how its ears are. If they appear to be burning, they will need some protection; do this by wrapping them in wet kitchen paper secured all around with scrumpled foil. These will be removed 20 minutes before the dish is ready.

After 4 hours of cooking, take the piglet out and check it. Slide a carving fork into its rear end haunch: it should crunch through the crackling, entering easily into the tender soft meat. If there is any obvious resistance to the meat near the centre it is not ready and should be returned to the oven and checked every half hour until it is. Take the piglet out, and place it on a platter if you wish. If you don't do this, make sure that around your carving area you have plenty of dishcloths, as the meat can be very juicy.

While the piglet rests, take the tray with the juices and pour off as much of the fat as you can (but not down the sink). Put the tray on the hob and turn the heat up high. Add the cider and rapidly simmer for about 5 minutes. Pour this juice into jugs and place them on the table for all to splash about their meat and stuffing.

Having always cooked this dish for New Year's Eve, my favourite presentation is to surround the piglet with holly, and to have five sparklers protruding from its back, lit just before I take the piglet to table. When everyone has seen it, carve off the meats and skin and arrange them on a large platter next to the spooned out stuffing. A huge sharp salad, containing lots of watercress, segmented oranges and raw shallot with a sharp vinaigrette is a good accompaniment to the moreish, fatty and most giving meats of the piglet.

NOTE: *For a 5kg piglet change the amounts, weights and volumes to: 2 onions, 25g butter, 1 tablespoon of finely chopped root ginger, a small handful of thyme, 200g black pudding, 2 Bramley apples, 1 x 200g bloomer loaf, a small handful of parsley, and 160ml dry cider. Cook the piglet at 190°C/375°F/Gas 5. After 2½ hours of cooking, loosely cover the piglet with foil. Check if it is ready after 3½-4 hours.*

HAM WITH AUTUMN VEGETABLES IN PARSLEY SAUCE

Before going to the white wall to await 'steady, aim, fire', I'm pretty sure that my last meal would be ham in parsley sauce. Of course the gaol cook would be excellent! It's hard to make this kind of decision – having eaten so many wonderful things I feel a traitor – but a plate of this dish, a glass of cider and the Sunday papers is simply unbeatable.

Serves 6-8

3 small onions
3 celery sticks
3 leeks
6 medium carrots
1 small swede
1 x 2kg uncooked, unsmoked ham
3 bay leaves
4 cloves

PARSLEY SAUCE
50g butter
75g plain flour
1 level teaspoon English mustard powder
200ml milk
1 heaped teaspoon wholegrain mustard
    (optional)
1 large bunch of fresh parsley

Clean the vegetables. Peel the onions and then halve them from top to bottom, leaving a little of the hard root end to ensure each half does not come apart. De-string and halve the celery sticks and cut the leeks across the middle too. Trim any tops from the carrots and leave them whole. Peel and chop the swede into six pieces.

Lower your ham into a good-sized flameproof pot that can comfortably accommodate the vegetables as well. Well cover with cold water and drop the vegetables in with the bay and cloves. Bring all this to a gentle simmer. Skim when necessary. Sitting on the top, it will need to cook for 2-2$^{1}/_{2}$ hours, lid off.

When the ham is cooked, turn off the heat and leave it to sit while you make the sauce. In a saucepan, melt the butter on a medium heat before stirring in the flour and mustard powder. Use a whisk, as it will help banish any lumps. Let this all foam, but do not let it colour! About 1 minute will be fine. Mix the milk and 500ml of the stock from the ham in a measuring jug. Add this bit by bit. The sauce will immediately clag up, but not to worry; just continue adding more liquid, as it will loosen. Stir in the grain mustard if you want it. Leave the sauce to slowly tick over on a light simmer.

Pick the parsley leaves and then finely chop them. Don't add them to the sauce until you are ready to eat, or they will turn a khaki colour.

Carve the ham and place it in the centre of a good-sized platter, surrounded by the soft vegetables. Once seated, lift these to the plates and blanket with the parsley sauce. If potatoes are required, I suggest boiled ones.

PORK, ANCHOVY AND BLACK OLIVE STEW ON POLENTA

Driving through a small hilltop village in Tuscany, surrounded by leafless chestnut woods and lost, grumpy, cold and hungry, I decided it was time to stop. I chose an empty establishment with pink tablecloths and floral-tiled walls. Once seated I received no menu, and it was clear there was no choice. You ate what you were given. 'Cinghiale,' said a stout, short woman, and I nodded. A dark stew was produced from a huge copper pan resting in the glowing hearth. Brought to the table, it was surrounded by fabulously rich, cheesy, bright yellow, wet polenta. With one mouthful my good humour was instantly restored.

As the place was empty I asked for a little more, which greatly pleased my proprietor. I then asked her about the great hound that lay in the corner and the terrifying fresh stitches in its flank. She said it was her husband's dog and had brought down the very brute I was eating. The boar had been slowed by a bullet, but as the dog was upon it, he had not escaped the goring tusks of this furious dying pig. My interest and appetite secured a couple of free grappas, and I was on my way. It had seemed like a good place to stop and it was. This translation of the recipe is not far off what I remember her telling me, and what I tasted. I've replaced boar with pork, but use boar if you can.

Serves 6-8

2kg boned pork or wild boar shoulder, skin removed
olive oil
1 large sprig fresh rosemary
$^1/_2$ head of garlic, cloves separated and peeled
12 good salted anchovies, in oil, drained
1 large white onion (brown will do), finely diced
2 medium fennel bulbs, finely diced
strips of rind and juice of $^1/_2$ lemon
1 x 75cl bottle Barolo or other Italian red

1 teaspoon cinnamon
1 tablespoon tomato purée
200g good bitter wrinkly little black olives, stoned
large-flaked sea salt and black pepper

TO SERVE
1 packet instant polenta
butter, olive oil and freshly grated Parmesan, to taste
a few handfuls gvremolata (chopped parsley, mixed with a little finely chopped garlic and grated lemon zest)

Preheat the oven to 200°C/400°F/Gas 6. Chop the meat into pieces the size of a child's fist, not including the rind.

Heat about half a wine glass of olive oil in a large lidded heavy pan with the rosemary sprig. When the oil is hot but not smoking, throw in all the cloves of garlic and the anchovies, stirring until the anchovies have collapsed and the garlic has browned. Add the onion and fennel, the large strips of peeled lemon rind and the juice. Cook on a moderate heat with the lid on until totally soft. Add the pork to the pot and stir through before adding the wine, cinnamon and tomato purée.

Put the lid on, put the pot into the preheated oven, and cook for 2 hours. Remove the lid and throw in the olives. Stir them through (tinny stoned olives simply will not do: they do not have enough attitude, bitterness, saltiness, or anything to remark on for that matter). Return the pot to the oven with the lid off, and cook for 20-30 minutes. This will reduce the sauce and intensify the dish, and you want the meat to be very tender. Season to taste.

About 15 minutes before serving would be a good time to make a wet polenta. The instant packets are perfectly respectable, but are made truly delicious with the addition of lots of butter, olive oil and grated Parmesan. (Follow the instructions on the packet, you don't need any more from me.)

When eating, you want three good yellow and sloppy spoonfuls of polenta with your intense dark pork stew in the middle. Scatter over a handful of *gvremolata*.

BEEF

CORNED BEEF HASH WITH BRUSSELS SPROUTS (OR NOT)

Boiled potatoes feature regularly in my tiny kitchen, so there are normally a few knocking around in the fridge at breakfast time. They are perfect for this recipe. The other main player is the corned beef, a love-it or hate-it thing (I know where my loyalties lie). Follow me those who care to read on. If you have any leftover sprouts, use them now. I start by frying the sprouts, as I like the taste of them when a little burnt. Sure you can have an egg on top, but I find it a little too much. I'll stick with a blob of ketchup. If you can't bear sprouts, use an onion or cabbage. Cook these too with a little burning.

Serves 2

400g boiled potatoes, or leftovers
200g raw or leftover Brussels sprouts
40g butter

large-flaked sea salt and black pepper
200g corned beef
1 good teaspoon made English mustard
150ml milk

If making this from scratch, boil the potatoes first and let them cool. Skin on or off, it's up to you. Make sure you don't boil them so much that they fall to pieces as you attempt to grate them. Medium potatoes cut into four pieces will take about 10 minutes in boiling water until ready.

If the sprouts are fresh, peel off any outer layer that needs removing and roughly slice them. Heat a big knob of the butter in a non-stick frying pan and hard-fry the fresh sprouts with salt, pepper and adding a splash of water if using fresh. Cook them fast until they begin to burn.

While they are cooking, cut the block of the corned beef into slices, crumble it roughly with your fingers and then add it to the sprouts. Reduce the heat to medium. Grate in the potatoes on the large kiddies' cheese kind of setting. After the potato has snowed all over the top, mix it through and check the seasoning. Take the rest of the butter, split it into little knobs and dot it around, pushing it through the hash to the base of the pan. Jiggle the pan to make sure the hash can shuffle a bit and will turn out.

Mix the mustard into the milk and pour it evenly around the hash. Leave the hash to cook now, undisturbed. When turned out it will be crisp on top and soft inside. Cook it on a medium to low heat until you get that nice crusty, slightly burnt smell, about 15-20 minutes. Check to see if it is ready by lifting one side with a spatula – it should be a caramel brown.

Either serve it from the pan or turn it out on a plate (I think this is nicer). Eat with as much ketchup as you please, washed down with coffee.

OXTAIL STEW

Rich, unctuous and meaty, sweetened with the sugar of roots and redcurrant jelly, this is my favourite stew. Navigating my way round the large jigsaw-puzzle bones to search out those tender, gluey mouthfuls, the person sitting next to me is left unanswered as I obsess silently over my plate. Heavy and hearty, there is no point in attempting to do much more after consuming oxtail other than ordering more pints of bitter in the local pub. Probably best eaten on Sundays.

Serves 6

6 large oxtail bones
2 level tablespoons plain flour
1 heaped teaspoon English mustard
    powder
large-flaked sea salt and black pepper
2 generous tablespoons dripping
2 large banana shallots, peeled and
    finely chopped
3 garlic cloves, peeled and finely chopped

leaves from a sprig of fresh thyme
3 bay leaves
6 cloves
freshly grated nutmeg
1 x 75cl bottle red wine
1 tablespoon tomato purée
$1/2$ medium swede
3 medium parsnips
4 medium carrots
2 tablespoons redcurrant jelly
a good handful of parsley, chopped

Preheat the oven to 180°C/350°F/Gas 4.

When selecting the oxtail from the butcher, choose the really thick parts, not the bits no bigger than the base of a whippet's tail.

Throw the plain flour, mustard powder and 1 tablespoon salt into a plastic bag. Add the oxtails and twist the bag closed, trapping a little air. Shake the bag around. The bones should be well coated in flour. Remove them from the bag.

Choose a lidded flameproof casserole big enough to fit all the oxtail in one even layer, plus the vegetables that will eventually join them, but not so large that, on pouring in the wine, the level has to be bumped up with water to cover the oxtails. Heat the dripping until the first traces of smoke are just discernible. Brown the oxtails all over. Do this thoroughly, which might be easier done in two batches. If at the end of the browning stage there are obvious burned bits in the pan, I would suggest you wipe them out with some kitchen paper, taking care not to burn yourself.

Return the oxtails to the pot with the shallots and garlic, the thyme, bay, cloves and a good grating of nutmeg. Pour the wine about: it should just cover the oxtail. Stir in the tomato purée. On the heat, bring everything up to a gentle simmer. If any scum drifts to the top, remove this now. Put the lid on and cook the oxtail in the preheated oven for $1 1/2$ hours.

When this time is up, remove the dish from the oven. You will notice that a lot of fat has come out of the oxtail and risen to the top. This needs to be removed, and you have two choices: if skimming it when hot, tilt the casserole at an angle and ladle out the fat; alternatively, if you let the pot sit on the window-sill, as soon as the stew has cooled, the fat will become opaque and can easily be scraped off (this is even easier to remove when left in the fridge). The longer this dish takes to sit at any point, the tastier it gets. I never hurry oxtail. I might make it over two days.

When skimmed of the fat, turn the oxtails over before poking in the swede, parsnips and carrots that you have peeled and chopped into 3cm batons. Plop in the redcurrant jelly and blast with a good grind of black pepper. Return the lid and cook for a further $1^1/2$ hours in the same temperature oven.

Remove the casserole, tilt it and skim out more fat, which will almost certainly have come to the top. Remove one piece of the oxtail and, targeting a meaty area, pull at it with a fork. If the meat comes away very easily, it is ready; if not, it must be returned to the oven. It will require a little longer; you must test it again.

Take the stew to the table, scattered all about with the chopped parsley. Because of all the roots within, I tend to eat the dish as is, with no extra vegetables, although mash is always a welcome guest.

RABBIT

It appears my family name was once entangled with rabbits like a bunny in a bramble hedge. Warner, it is thought, derives from Warrener, a rabbit keeper or game warden. Once upon a time rabbits were highly prized, as they were scarce in mainland Britain, preferring the sandier soils of our shores and isles. Warreners would lay clay pipes in the ground, raising rabbits in these artificial burrows for the high table. Rabbits are cheap and can be very tasty. They must be cooked slowly or be very young, as, unlike larger white rabbits reared for the European pot or the dark depths of Magic Marvin's hat, they have next to no fat. Reared rabbits are easier to cook, but lack the delicious hint of grasses. Rabbits are good from autumn to late spring. The adults should be avoided during the breeding. Any small rabbit can be fried, whereas larger rabbits require a lower oven temperature and patience.

RABBIT WITH PETITS POIS, CIDER AND LETTUCE

Apart from being delicious, the other thing that gives me great satisfaction from this dish that a rabbit ends up in the pot with the very same things it has dedicated itself to stealing from your garden. One thing to remember about wild rabbits is that they have done a lot of scampering around and contain very little fat, therefore gentle heat and slow cooking are required. If it's possible, order rabbits that have been shot with a rifle, as less damage is caused to the meat than from the scatter of a shotgun. Choose medium-sized rabbits, as old ones can be a little gnarly.

You may think it rather odd to be cooking lettuces, but it works surprisingly well.

Serves 6

2 rabbits
1 tablespoon plain flour (optional)
large-flaked sea salt and black pepper
3 medium shallots
2 garlic cloves
4 nice carrots
2 celery sticks
450g smoked lardons
butter

olive oil
2 bay leaves
freshly grated nutmeg, to taste
3 sprigs of fresh thyme, leaves picked
1 x 660ml bottle French or good dry
    farmhouse cider
2 x 410g tins petits pois
1 heaped tablespoon Dijon mustard
50ml red wine vinegar
1 small cos lettuce or 2 little gem lettuces
a large handful of mint

Preheat the oven to 190°C/375°F/Gas 5.

Joint the rabbit, or have it done for you by the butcher. Each rabbit should break into six pieces: two back legs, two front legs and two saddle parts. Discard the ribcage or keep it for stock. You now have two options: should you want to flour the rabbit pieces, the sauce will be thicker; the other option is not to flour, in which case the sauce will be thinner. If you do choose to, pop all the rabbit pieces in a plastic bag with the flour and a good tablespoon of salt. (Don't worry about the amount of salt; some will be left in the bottom of the bag.) Trap some air in the bag and shake it around, making sure that the bag is strong, or as if by magic your rabbit will disappear in a puff of white – on to the floor.

Before using the rabbit, get all the vegetables and lardons ready so that all the cooking can be done in a relatively fluid process. Peel the shallots, garlic and carrots and string the celery. Dice all of these up nice and small and mix with the lardons in a bowl. Leave to one side.

Heat a large knob of butter in the base of a lidded flameproof casserole big enough to fit all the rabbit pieces in. You are going to brown the rabbit in two batches. Don't cram it all in at once, or you won't get the desired colour. If you put it in a pot that is not hot enough it will sit there miserably, slowly coming up to heat, and it will toughen. You want this process to happen quickly.

When the butter is turning nut brown, throw in half the rabbit pieces; if they are unfloured you need to salt them. Don't jiggle them around but leave them to pick up colour. After 2 minutes, turn the pieces over and brown the other side. Remove the pieces and repeat the process with the remaining rabbit. You might need to add another knob of butter. Remove the rabbit to a plate. Add 2 tablespoons of water to stop the 'catchings' from burning.

Throw in the vegetables and lardons, adding a little splash of olive oil to get them going, along with the bay leaves, nutmeg and thyme, sweating them gently for about 20 minutes until you detect a tenderness. Nestle the rabbit pieces among the vegetables and pour in as much cider as is needed to cover them. Add the peas from both tins, but the juice from only one.

Put the pot in the preheated oven and cook, covered, for 1 hour. Remove the pot from the oven and stir in the Dijon mustard and red wine vinegar. If there's a dryness on top, add a splash more cider. Return to the oven for another hour. Remove and put on a medium heat on the hob. Take off the lid.

Chop your clean lettuce into 2cm ribbons from stem to tip, and cut yourself a large knob of fridge-cold butter. Rip up a good handful of mint, ideally the tough little English varieties growing by the back door, which are better that the big floppy ones from the supermarket. Throw the butter and lettuce in with the rabbit and stir it all through. As soon as the leaf of the lettuce has wilted, but the stalk is still obviously crisp, it is ready to be served. If the cooking pot is ugly, transfer to a nice serving dish, and scatter the mint over the top. Eat with boiled potatoes or a good, creamy mash (*see* page 191).

POT BRAISED RABBIT AND FENNEL

This recipe was a most happy accident, the result of a morning's tinkering under the influence of the two-coffee fidgets (and the resulting failure to do any of the work I needed to do). The ingredients used comprised bits, bobs and cut-offs strewn across the kitchen. On gathering them all up, I decided to purée the lot and slap it on a couple of wee bunnies and roast them in a pot. The result, I think, is excellent.

Serves 4

1 young rabbit
1 big sprig of fresh rosemary
8 fresh sage leaves
4 big generous sprigs of thyme
4 good garlic cloves

1 whole small fennel bulb and its top
2 dried hot bird's eye chillies
juice of 1 medium lemon
50ml extra virgin olive oil
2 teaspoon large-flaked sea salt

TO SERVE
a small handful of parsley leaves
top-quality extra virgin olive oil

Preheat the oven to 170°C/325°F/Gas 3.

When you are choosing your rabbit pick the smallest, as it will be more tender. Have the rabbit cut into six pieces, and keep the ribcage to use for stock. Rinse and drain the rabbit pieces and place in a bowl.

Strip the rosemary, sage and thyme from their stalks, peel the garlic and roughly chop the whole fennel. Put all the ingredients bar the rabbit in a blender. Blitz the lot into a purée. Spoon this over the rabbit pieces, making sure all is well mixed.

For cooking the rabbit, ideally you want a small, lidded earthenware pot that the ingredients should fit snugly into. Choose something similar in size if you don't have one to hand, but the heavier the dish is the better. Pack the rabbit into the pot, scraping the rest of the purée over the top. Add 100ml water and put on the lid.

Cook the rabbit in the preheated oven for 2 hours. Remove the lid and poke a fork into the rabbit meats, which should be very soft. Serve the rabbit portions in bowls, scattered with some parsley and drizzled with a little olive oil. This dish is excellent eaten with some fried potatoes.

LEFTOVERS: *Pick any remaining meat from the rabbit bones into little mouthfuls and place them in a bowl with some boiled green beans and shaved raw fennel. Mix some of the leftover sauce into a vinaigrette with a dollop of Dijon mustard, sugar and lemon juice to taste and some good olive oil. Add to the meat and vegetables and mix gently. This makes a good dish for any remaining hot days.*

HARE

On a freezing cold Saturday, I was returning from a walk with my father. We were weary but lost in chat, and descended the steep Berkshire downs to the chalk and flint below. It was here, in the middle of a field, that we came upon a sight of unnerving peculiarity. Nine hares were seated in a perfect circle, each one facing inwards. Within the circle were two hares back to back, facing what may have been their jury, pupils or tribe. Hair prickling, we walked slowly forward and, disturbed by our intrusion, the gathering broke and each cantered off with a slight look of annoyance. We faced each other, placing our hands on one another's shoulders, and agreed that we really had both seen the same peculiar sight. Dusk felt witchier, and we walked home in awe-struck silence. I will no longer lift the gun to a hare as I am convinced that they have access to nature's secrets. I still occasionally sit down to a plate of hare, finding its seductive smell and dark meat irresistible.

GOOD HARE

This is one of my favourite dishes in late autumn/winter; the meat tastes at its best from September to February. It's simple but must be cooked with care.

Serves 6

1 large hare, hung (preferably not frozen), cleaned, jointed, blood reserved
duck fat
1 heaped tablespoon plain flour
1 heaped teaspoon ground ginger
large-flaked sea salt and black pepper
8 rashers of rindless smoked streaky bacon
2 medium white onions, peeled and chopped
3 garlic cloves, peeled and crushed
5 medium carrots, chopped
2 celery sticks, de-stringed and chopped
3 big fresh bay leaves
6 cloves
an enthusiastic grating of nutmeg
1 x 75cl bottle red wine (Bordeaux or Côtes du Rhône) or 2 x 500ml cans good brown ale
peeled rind and juice of $1/2$ small lemon
2 tablespoons redcurrant jelly
1 teaspoon unsweetened cocoa powder
1 capful red wine vinegar
a fistful of finely chopped fresh parley

Have your butcher chop the hare into nine pieces. Both back legs should be cut into two, the saddle into two, the front legs left whole. The ninth piece is above the saddle but includes the ribcage. Have the ribs cut away, leaving one more meaty back piece, avoiding these ribs falling into the stew later.

Preheat the oven to 180°C/350°F/Gas 4. Choose a big, lidded flameproof casserole and get 2 tablespoons of duck fat in and heating up.

Rinse the hare, making sure stray fur is washed off. Place the flour, ginger, a large pinch of salt and the hare in a plastic bag. Twist the top closed with some air trapped inside and shake. Choose a strong bag, or prepare to witness the hare bolt.

The fat must be hot, as the hare needs to be browned fast. Don't rush. Place the flour-coated pieces in the sizzling fat and fry, turning the pieces once on each side, until the meat is browned. Transfer to a plate. Turn down the heat and add a little more fat. Then add the bacon, vegetables, bay, cloves, nutmeg and 1 tablespoon salt, sweating until soft, 15-20 minutes.

Add the hare pieces back to the pot and pour in the wine or $1^1/_2$ cans of the ale with the lemon rind and juice. Put the lid on and put the pot in the oven and cook for 2 hours. Stir in the redcurrant jelly, then return the lid and cook for another hour. Remove the lid and, with a carving fork or tip of a knife, poke a piece of hare. The point should move into the meat easily with only the slightest resistance. When eating, the meat should come away easily with a fork but not be collapsing off the bone unprompted.

Mix the cocoa, red wine vinegar and blood (if using) into a paste. Put the pot on a low heat on the hob and stir in the blood mixture to thicken the sauce. Cook at the gentlest simmer for 5 minutes. The hare is ready.

Sprinkle with the well chopped parsley and serve the hare with some red cabbage (*see* page 172) and potato purée (*see* page 191) or boiled potatoes. Wash it down with the remaining ale or a good red wine.

LEFTOVERS: *Take the meat off the bone and add to the leftover sauce. Heat while cooking some tagliatelle. Drain the pasta and mix into the hare sauce. Serve in a bowl, adding a little olive oil, a good scattering of grated Parmesan and some more chopped parsley.*

VENISON

The red deer is naturally a woodland animal and forced into the glens. Scottish deer are smaller than their southern cousins. I have spent happy days stalking the red and the roe, huffing and puffing through the heather, surrounded by staggering beauty untainted by the swoosh of cars. Shooting a deer is no light-hearted matter, but when the bullet has acted swiftly and the deer has been gralloched and taken from the hill, one becomes aware of the reverential hush this pursuit commands. So much observation is necessary to understand and maintain the herds and, coupled with such a strong code of practice, it is hard to suggest any lack of respect for the animal – a respect that can only be followed by a quiet thank you, whispered in the wind. Given the choice, I prefer get my meat this way than to point at the glass of the butcher's counter.

LEBANESE-STYLE VENISON SANDWICH

After a night out in London, when I get peckish around 3am, I skip to the Edgware Road and get involved with a tasty lamb sandwich. The following recipe uses red deer fillet, which is an excellent replacement. Although there seem to be many parts to this recipe, it is very quick and easy to prepare.

Makes 3-4

500g venison fillet
1 tablespoon cumin seeds
4 tablespoons olive oil
1 fresh red chilli
1 x 400g tin chopped tomatoes
1 cinnamon stick, snapped in two
1 teaspoon caster sugar
large-flaked sea salt and black pepper

juice of 1 lemon
3 tablespoons shop-bought mayonnaise
3 garlic cloves, finely diced
3 pickled cucumbers
12-16 fresh mint leaves
1 red onion, skinned and thinly sliced
½ small white cabbage, washed and
   shredded

TO SERVE
3-4 *khobz* (Lebanese flatbreads), or pitta

Roughly dice the venison into mouth-sized chunks and mix it with the cumin seeds and 2 tablespoons olive oil. Cover and leave to one side.

Finely dice the chilli, and fry it with the remaining olive oil until it's lighter in colour, about 2 minutes. Flop a little more than half the tin of tomatoes in and add the cinnamon. Add the sugar, a good pinch of salt and the juice of half the lemon. Bubble gently on a low heat for half an hour. Turn the heat off, remove the cinnamon and blitz with a stick blender. Let it cool.

Combine the mayonnaise with the garlic, the remaining lemon juice and 2 teaspoons water. Mix and put to one side. Chop each pickled cucumber into six lengths and put them on a plate with four mint leaves per sandwich, the onion and cabbage. You have now prepared all the fillings.

Tear greaseproof paper to A3 size sheets. Turn the oven on to a low heat to warm the *khobz* or otherwise pitta bread. Get a large dry frying pan extremely hot but do not add any oil; colouring should occur quickly.

Add salt to the meat and mix it before casting the venison into the hot pan to sizzle violently. Stir, ensuring that all the pieces cook evenly. Providing the pan is big enough, the meat will be medium-rare after about 4-5 minutes.

Place the *khobz* in the centre of the paper. Line up six to seven pieces of meat slightly off its centre. Add cucumber, mint, red onion and cabbage and 3 teaspoons of each sauce. Remember not to over-fill. Roll the bread before rolling in the paper as tightly as possible. When half rolled, fold in the right side end and then keep rolling. This will stop the contents from leaking when eating. When fully rolled, twist the open end like a sweetie wrapper and give to someone to tear open the top and attack. (Filling pitta is pretty obvious; after warming, stuff, wrap and tear open as you see fit.)

VENISON PIE

When I'm holed up in the countryside I like to cook as simply as possible, partly because in the most remote village shops asking for cumin or olive oil can get you the same look as wearing a leotard in the high street. The following ingredients shouldn't raise any eyebrows. Use the shoulder or leg for this recipe as the saddle is too lean and should be kept for cooking rare. I don't like swamping deer meat in boozy marinades as the taste gets lost. Leave the lid off and make a good stew.

Serves 4-6

1kg shoulder or leg of red deer venison
40g dripping
2 large onions, peeled and finely diced
1 heaped tablespoon plain flour
1 teaspoon English mustard powder
4 medium carrots, peeled and diced
1 x 500ml can dark ale
1 tablespoon soft brown sugar
3 tablespoons malt vinegar

a heavy grating of nutmeg
1 big sprig of fresh thyme
large-flaked sea salt and a good blast of
    black pepper
2 ginger biscuits

TOPPING
1 portion rough puff pastry (*see* page 249)
plain flour, for dusting
1 medium egg, beaten with 1 tablespoon
    milk

Have the butcher cut the venison into proper over-sized mouthfuls that might need cutting once on your plate, as these cook better than small chunks.

Preheat the oven to 180°C/350°F/Gas 4. Heat the dripping in a large, lidded flameproof casserole on the hob and add the onions, frying them until they are soft and browned. Turn off the heat and sift the flour and mustard powder into the pot. Stir until you have a thickish onion mix. Add the meat and carrots and stir into the onions. (You are not pre-browning the meat, as with venison this makes it clench like a fist.) Add the ale, sugar, vinegar, nutmeg, thyme and pepper, and both ginger biscuits, finely grated. Stir once more. Do not add any salt; you'll do this at the end. Cover the contents of the pot with a circle of neatly cut greaseproof and put the lid on, then cook it in the preheated oven for $1^1/_2$ hours. When the time is up, add a tablespoon of salt.

Transfer the contents of the casserole to a pie dish. Use a deep dish, as a wide shallow one will have the pie crust drooping in the middle, thus becoming soggy. Turn the temperature of the oven up to 200°C/400°F/Gas 6.

Roll your pastry out to a thickness of about 7mm and lay it over your unctuous deer filling. Leave a slight overhang and crimp the edges with a fork. Paint the top of your pie evenly with the beaten egg and milk. This is the time to fashion any pastry motif appropriate to the occasion and place it on top. Prick a hole in the middle of the pastry, no larger than a wren's eye.

Cook for 40-45 minutes, until the pastry is a rich hazelnut brown. If in doubt, cook a little longer, as pale, soggy pastry is not as pleasing. Dive in.

Val Weaver

PLUMP BIRDS

CHICKEN

CHICKEN WITH CEP SAUCE

Finding any mushroom is like finding treasure. But it is the cep or penny bun that I prize most highly. Searching the damp moss or concealing grasses or peering beneath the silver birches, on finding them I feel total jubilation. It is obvious why the penny bun has its name, the cap looking like a large, warm, fresh-baked bread roll.

In this recipe, I would advocate using good quality mushrooms. But if yours are inflicted with insect damage and there are visible signs of attack, gently bump the stalk on a board to dislodge any wee grubs from their favourite restaurant. It's not worth making a fuss over one or two left inside; after all, you're all eating the same thing.

I'm writing this for two, as you won't always return home with a basket containing as many of these mushrooms as you would like.

Serves 2

2 free-range chicken legs
olive oil
large-flaked sea salt and black pepper

CEP SAUCE
200g fresh penny bun or cep mushrooms, cleaned
2 tablespoons vermouth
50ml good chicken stock (*see* page 246)
1 heaped teaspoon tomato purée
20g fridge-cold butter

Preheat the oven to 230°C/450°F/Gas 8.

Rub the chicken legs all over with olive oil before seasoning them generously with some salt and pepper. Heat a non-stick oven-proof frying pan or thick non-stick oven tray over a medium-high heat until it is very hot, so that when the chicken hits the surface you know that you are frying. Sizzle, sizzle.

Keeping the legs skin-side down, fry for about 10 minutes, turning them once or twice to achieve a lovely even browning. While they are frying, cut the ceps into big flat slices, taking efforts to retain their shape – this is easier with firm specimens.

When the chicken is good and coloured, pour off half the collected fat. Arrange the mushroom slices around the legs, turning them over so they pick up the remaining rendered chicken fat in the pan. Pop the pan in the oven and cook for 15 minutes. When the chicken is done, remove the pan from the oven (remembering the handle will be violently hot). Check it is cooked by pushing a skewer into the leg at the thickest point; if the juices run clear it is cooked, if not give it another 2-3 minutes and then try again. If the mushrooms appear to be uncoloured, flip them over and you will see that the side facing down is a delightful orangey brown. Divide the chicken between two well warmed plates and cover with foil while you work quickly on your sauce.

Put the pan on the hob and turn it on to a high heat. Splash the vermouth over the mushrooms; it will evaporate almost immediately. Pour over the chicken stock and stir in the tomato purée, pushing against the bottom of the pan to mix the sticky chicken 'catchings' into the sauce. Boil hard for 3-4 minutes; the liquid should reduce by half. Check the seasoning.

Add the cold butter, chopped into little cubes, gradually to the pan, swirling all the time. This encourages the sauce to emulsify. When the sauce is nice and glossy and has thickened up, pour it around the chicken legs and eat immediately.

POACHED CHICKEN WITH BEETROOT AND HORSERADISH RELISH

I have noticed that for many in the UK the suggestion of poaching a chicken is met with a frown, perhaps because of the mistaken idea of some poor fowl bumping around in furiously boiling water. I urge you to try it. You will change sides. It is the first thing I will cook on returning from a holiday abroad and the first thing I'll cook when needing alternative medicine for a piggish cold. It is cheering with its warm broth and clean tastes, especially when I've had a few hard-core eating sessions in a row, but still want more meat. As autumn slips into winter, just change the vegetables as you see fit.

Serves 4

1 x 1.5kg free-range chicken
4 medium carrots
4 Jerusalem artichokes
4 garlic cloves
2 onions
1 small celeriac
3 celery sticks
2 leeks
2 teaspoons celery salt
large-flaked salt and black pepper

2 bay leaves
$^1/_2$ cinnamon stick

BEETROOT AND HORSERADISH RELISH

2 fresh medium beetroots, boiled for 1 hour
1 heaped teaspoon hot horseradish sauce, or 1 heaped tablespoon grated fresh horseradish
1 heaped teaspoon Dijon mustard
juice of $^1/_2$ lemon
3 tablespoons olive oil

Take a large lidded pot, big enough to accommodate the chicken and vegetables, and lower the chicken into the middle.

Peel the carrots and artichokes, leaving them whole. Peel the garlic and onions: cut the onions in half, leaving a little of the root end, as this will help keep each half reasonably intact. Peel the celeriac well and cut it into six pieces. De-string the celery and wash and trim the leeks. Cut both in half.

Place the vegetables and garlic around the chicken in the pot, evenly mixed up. Fill with water until the chicken is just submerged. It is important to note here that if you choose a pan that is too big you will have to add a lot more water, thereby diluting what would otherwise be a stronger, tastier stock. Add the celery salt, some black pepper, the bay and cinnamon.

Bring the chicken to a gentle simmer, cover, then cook it for 1 hour in total. Remember that once the lid is on, the temperature will increase: check that it is really simmering well and not now boiling. After 20 minutes, remove the lid and skim off any scum that has risen to the top. Return the lid for the rest of the cooking time.

Now it's time for the relish. Peel and grate both the beetroots on the large hole setting of your grater. Use rubber gloves, or notice everyone staring at your hands on public transport. Add the horseradish, mustard, a good grind of black pepper and 1 teaspoon salt, the lemon juice and the olive oil.

When you're ready to eat, take the chicken out of the stock. Check it is cooked by pushing a skewer into the thigh at the thickest point: if the juices run clear it is cooked; if not, give it another 10 minutes and then try again. Roughly carve it up; I don't like thin slices of chicken breast for this, I like big fat ones. Put it in the centre of a platter and surround with all the hot steaming vegetables. Place the platter on the table, allowing people to take what they want. Serve the soup in a mug or bowl alongside the chicken. Taste it first: it might need remastering with a little salt.

Do it how you will, but I tend to put the beetroot relish well to the side of the plate, as I like to see all the pale colours of the vegetables rather than a whole plate of techno pink. It goes very well, though.

LEFTOVERS: *For a reassuring chicken noodle soup, chop everything down to a smaller size. Reintroduce the vegetables to the broth, and the kernels of a fresh cob of sweetcorn and some broken vermicelli. Heat the stock and simmer until the pasta is soft. Add the chopped chicken at the end to avoid overcooking. Return to bed with hankies and your chicken doctor.*

PARTRIDGE

There are two species of partridge to be seen hopping and dashing full-tilt across the stubble, and they are the 'introduced' French or red-leg and the 'native' English or grey partridge. Because of the criminal and savage mauling of our hedgerows, we have seen a sad and dramatic demise of the English partridge, and the welcome refusal of many guns to shoot them in areas where their population has collapsed.

The two varieties have different habits. The English partridges, grey with a buff orange bib, stick together in diligent little groups called coveys, often seen sitting in a circle with unwinking sentries facing all directions on fox and hawk duty. The Frenchies, typically well dressed in scarlet trousers and stripy jackets, move in smaller groups of rarely more than five, and in flight they shift a little faster. Reared for shooting and less dependent on the hedgerow, they are abundant and are notably brighter than the pheasant.

For those who do enjoy shooting, partridges are an exciting quarry, zipping out of nowhere to burst over the hedge tops, wings birring before changing gear into a fast glide tipping left, right and away into the distance.

Partridge is a plump and tasty bird, juicier than the pheasant and, when hung properly, meltingly tender. For those not keen on a gamey twang, they make a good choice. Whether simply roasted with butter or braised with lentils, partridges are eye-rollingly delicious and regular guests in my flat.

PARTRIDGES WITH RAZ EL HANOUT

Tasted in a riad (a Moroccan guesthouse) in Marrakech, this dish was brought to me by a beautiful and proud-looking Berber woman. I ate it by a crackling fire, December being cold in the Atlas Mountains. I'll never forget the excitement I felt on eating this dish for the first time, then made with chicken.

Although butter will suffice for this dish, you will be closer to the real thing using ghee, which is readily available in many Indian markets. *Smen*, the Moroccan version, is harder to find (notably a little more rancid in taste) but use this if you can find it. Ideally, the preparation of the birds (or lamb) you are using should be done a day before you plan to cook the dish.

Serves 6

6 French (red-leg) partridges, which have been hung properly, plucked and cleaned
7 heaped teaspoons raz el hanout (*see* page 250, 1 per bird and 1 for the pot)
2 good fistfuls of sultanas (ideally yellow)

250ml water
3 medium red onions, peeled
80g butter or ghee
2 generous tablespoons runny honey (wildflower, mountain, thyme or acacia)
large-flaked sea salt
3 large eggs

The day before you plan to eat, place the partridges in a large bowl and cover them with their measure of raz el hanout. Rub the mix into their bodies with the same care you would expect from a massage administered by a loved one. Don't neglect the cavity and apply some of your blend inside. Cover the birds and put them in the fridge overnight. Soak the sultanas in the water in a bowl.

On the day of cooking, preheat the oven to **220°C/425°F/Gas 7**.

Take a large tagine or a heavy casserole big enough to fit your covey of partridges. Chop the red onions to as small as you can. Cast the onion into the pot and dot it with **10** or so pinched-off pieces of butter or ghee. Sit the birds side by side on top of the raw onion and scatter the soaked sultanas around, pouring in their water as well. Put the remaining knobs of butter all about the birds, then trail the honey over them, and pinch over a good **2** teaspoons salt. Put the lid on and cook in the preheated oven for **20** minutes. Turn down the heat to **180°C/350°F/Gas 4** and cook for another **20** minutes, having basted the birds with the juices. Check they are cooked and if not give them another **5-10** minutes. The breast meat closest to the bone should be pale pink.

Meanwhile, hard-boil the eggs, then cool, peel and halve them.

Take the pot out of the oven and put in the halved hard-boiled eggs. Cover the pot and leave to stand for **10** minutes. Serve immediately, a partridge per person, with sauce all about it and half an egg. Accompany with bread or couscous. Moroccan bread is hard to find in England unless you live in a North African neighbourhood. Where I live the Moroccans often eat this style of dish with ordinary soft white rolls baked until warm and just crisp.

CORONATION PARTRIDGE SANDWICH

Many find Coronation Chicken an absurd joke of the past, but it's my favourite sandwich filling, and this is my book and it's going in. By the end of the season, there are a lot of partridges knocking around in the freezer, feeling hurt and ignored. I hope they don't find it an indignity to be included in this outdated recipe.

The following can be eaten as a salad or packed between layers of good chewy, malty brown bread.

Serves 2

4 slices of bread
butter

PARTRIDGE FILLING
1 partridge
1 big celery stick
1 apple

1 tablespoon lemon juice
a small handful of raisins (or sultanas)
3 heaped tablespoons shop-bought
    mayonnaise
1 good heaped teaspoon curry powder
1/2 teaspoon English mustard powder
large-flaked sea salt and black pepper

Preheat the oven to 190°C/375°F/Gas 5.

Roast the partridge for 15-20 minutes, or until the legs are cooked through, before taking it out of the oven and allowing it to cool.

In the meantime, de-string and wash the celery and peel and core the apple. Cut the apple into pieces about the size of a half sugar lump, and sprinkle with lemon juice. Cut the celery into thin slivers. Pour a little hot water over the raisins or sultanas and leave to hydrate.

Spoon the mayonnaise into a bowl, and throw in the apple pieces. Add the celery and the drained raisins. Add the curry and mustard powders, season to taste with salt and pepper and stir everything together.

Peel the skin from the partridge and discard it. Chop the flesh into good juicy, bite-sized chunks – not too small, though – really making sure that you have taken all the meat off, not just most of it. Do you really need to eat any of the partridge now? It is exactly the right amount for the filling. Mix into the mayonnaise, and let it stand for about half an hour, so that the committee members can come to an agreement.

Slice and butter some bread, although I would say that I am quite partial to a sliced bag loaf for this affair. Then whop in your filling – I lean to the side of heavy loading.

PHEASANT CURRY

At the end of the game season I'm pheasanted out. Some birds will have been delicious, others dry and tough. By January, though, most birds – especially the cocks – are pretty gnarly. Many theories on the right approach to cooking tender pheasant have been written. I say get the pheasant in a curry.

English variations on curry would have most Indians howling with laughter, but I picked up the idea for this recipe when fishing in the Himalayas, where one by one our crate of scrawny live chickens went nobly to the pot. I am replacing chicken with pheasant, but the method is the same, bones 'n' all.

This recipe can be as hot as you like. Personally, I like to eat my food without chilli violence, loss of hearing and deep panic. This north-east Indian version should be mild and eaten with the stickier rice you find as you head into Burma. If at the end of autumn you find yourself with a lot of big tough spinach, keep the stems, don't bin them. Wash and chop them into 5cm lengths and add them to the curry 5 minutes before the end of cooking. They are a great alternative to the jungle greens I ate in this dish.

Serves 2

1 pheasant, preferably hen
1 medium onion
1 heaped teaspoon large-flaked sea salt
1 hot red chilli, chopped
2 small hot green chillies, or to taste
1 big thumb-sized piece of root ginger
2 garlic cloves
40g ghee or clarified butter (*see* page 216)

1 level tablespoon ground turmeric
6 cloves
1 cinnamon stick
1 enthusiastic grating of nutmeg
1 teaspoon celery salt
1 teaspoon ground cumin
seeds from 10 cardamom pods
a lot of black pepper
1 x 400ml tin coconut milk
big spinach stems (if available)

Ask your butcher to divide your pheasant through the centre, trim off the length of backbone of each half and cut off the legs. Leaving the meat on the bones, take a large knife and roughly chop each leg into four pieces. You can help the knife with a tap on top of the blade from a hammer or bust-up rolling pin. Do the same to both breast pieces. Put the meat to one side.

Skin and cut the onion into four and put it in a food processor with the salt and chillies. Peel the ginger and garlic and add these. Blitz to superfine.

Heat the ghee or butter in a large balti, wok or saucepan. When it is very hot, add the onion mix and pheasant. The pan needs to be big enough to freely stir the contents. Stir until it starts to take on colour. Mix in the turmeric, cloves, cinnamon, nutmeg, celery salt, cumin and cardamom seeds. Grind in lots of pepper and cook for another minute or so. Turn down the heat and pour in the coconut milk and 200ml water, not letting them rise above a faint simmer. Cook, lid on, for $1^1/_2$ hours. 5 minutes before the end add the spinach stems. Serve with nothing but sticky Thai rice or basmati if needs be.

DUCK

Looking upon the picked-over wreckage, chin oiled and shining, I think duck is one of the finest meats known to man, and that a distant quack from a nearby pond is enough to make me feel hungry. Crispy skin, luxurious fat, plump livers, pink juicy breasts peaking through vinegared leaves, grilled hearts and a stock for the finest soups – my duck love is unconditional. So versatile and with so many treats to offer up, I eat the duck's meats in the consolation that nothing will be wasted. I will never cook a duck carelessly, for a dead duck in feather is a sad thing. Its svelte plumage, head drooping as if in sleep, invokes in me a sense of tragedy not matched by the sight of, say, a dead pheasant.

The wild and the tamed duck are two very different things. Farmed duck, available all year round, is more versatile than its wild cousin and has a greater yield of meat, fat and other usables. It is bigger, has done little other than waddle about and has been provided with a continuous diet of corn and wheat. It is wonderful, but its provenance is for you to find out and make your decision upon. The wild duck, on the other hand, will be hunted along the shore, river and lakeside. They are very active birds and will have used their wings a lot. Eating weeds, insects and small fish, their taste is earthier, the meat darker and gamier, intensified by the necessity to hang it.

In cooking as well as in taste, the differences are huge. Ducks can be tricky to cook sometimes and, apart from the teal, I would say are better cooked off the bone, as this will allow you to keep the breast pink. (By the time the legs are ready, the breast would be dry.) It also allows the skin to crisp and cease being like chewing on a rubber glove. Long, slow cooking is best kept for hand-reared ducks.

So why bother? Given the right treatment they are delicious. There is only a certain time of year in which wild ducks may be eaten (September 1st to February 1st) and so I like to enjoy them while I can. Because I hunt them, there is little reason to buy a reared one, unless my duck fat reserves are looking worryingly low or a recipe that dictates farmed duck. Those long-alone times, hunkered behind a hedge as the last light of day clings to the hill, when all is silence and silhouettes, waiting for the tell-tale squeak of those racing wings, only make this wonderful meat better. Many a good time I've had sitting down to a roasted wild duck with fork, pocket knife and bottle of good red wine.

DUCK CONFIT

Definitely one of my favourite ways to eat duck, it is that combination of crispy skin, soft and tender strings of meat and the joyous saltiness that makes duck confit so utterly delicious. When eating confit, it is best coupled with some element of sharpness to cut through the fattiness like the tip of Zorro's sword. Two suggestions I would advocate are marrow with caraway (*see* page 167) and sauerkraut with apples (*see* page 72).

Making confit can be a very neat and tidy process or one where you are skidding about in duck fat. The choice is yours. Be mindful not to block your sink when washing up, as, coupled with cold water, the fat will do the same in your drain as it might do in a gourmand's arteries.

Serves 8

8 good farmed-duck legs
20 black peppercorns, broken
8 sprigs of fresh thyme

8 sprigs of fresh rosemary
16 juniper berries
rock salt
750g duck fat
125ml decent white wine

For stage one, choose a container that can hold the ducks in two layers comfortably. In the bottom of this, chuck all the peppercorns, herbs and juniper berries plus 1 heaped tablespoon rock salt per duck leg. Add the duck legs and turn everything over together, really rubbing in the salt. Get some order in the container and stack the duck legs in two layers, making sure all the salt and aromatics are not just on the bottom of the container but distributed evenly throughout. Put the lid on and store this in the fridge for one day minimum, ideally two.

On the day you plan to cook the legs – stage two – take them out of the container and brush off all the salt and herbs. Put them to one side. Gently melt the duck fat in a heavy-based saucepan in which the duck legs will be a snug fit. Add the legs. Top it up with any extra duck fat you may; the bigger the pan, the more you will need. Pour over the white wine; the legs should be just submerged. Cut a circle of greaseproof paper that fits neatly inside the pot on top of the confit. Bring the legs to the faintest 'plup, plup, plup' bubble and leave the pot on this heat to cook.

I will not give you specific timings here, as you must test the meat; it will take between 2 and 2$^1/_2$ hours to cook. When you want to test the confit, take a piece from the fat using some tongs and put it on to a plate. The meat should almost fall away, but with a little prompting, not of its own accord. When they are ready, take all the legs out, put them in a sealable container and cover with the duck fat, once it has cooled. Preserved like this you can keep these legs in the fridge for a couple of months.

Now for stage three. When you are ready to use the legs, take the required amount and scrape off the fat. Turn the oven on to full blast. Place the duck confit in a totally metal frying pan or oven tray and put it in the preheated oven. Cook it for 15 minutes before having a look. When done, it will be dark brown, sizzling and crisp. *Joy*!

When removing confit legs to the plate, hold the pan or tray with an oven cloth and lift them with a spatula, as they can tend to stick if non-stick ware has not been used.

NOTE: *With wild ducks, collect the legs and freeze them over the season. Defrost them in February and confit a big batch. For the wild duck legs, you only need $^1/_2$ tablespoon rock salt per leg. You will need to eat three per sitting. Hardly a problem.*

LE GARBURE

This is a most delicious soup from the south-west of France. Very easy to assemble, it will provide you with a bolstering feast, arriving as a fine plate of poached meats and vegetables, accompanied by a bowl of tasty broth, or sometimes all in together. As always, there are those who say it must be made in a particular way – to which I would reply 'Go and boil your head'. If I want pumpkin in mine then I shall. I've wolfed Garbure in many places and each time found it filled with different vegetables that regionally show their smooth or knobbly faces, or are prevalent at a certain time of year. Certainly, four allies I always like to see in this dish are Savoy cabbage, haricot beans, a smoked pig of some description and duck or goose confit. By all means change the root vegetables, but remember that some will require less cooking, especially marrow and pumpkin.

Serves 6-8

200g white haricot beans, rinsed
3 litres water
2 medium onions
4 cloves
2-3 sprigs of fresh thyme
3 fresh bay leaves
large-flaked sea salt and black pepper
$^1/_2$ teaspoon freshly grated nutmeg

6 garlic cloves
700g smoked whole bacon or smoked uncooked ham hock (order them from your butcher)
4 medium carrots
4 medium turnips
$^1/_2$ swede
3 medium leeks
$^1/_2$ Savoy cabbage
4 confit duck legs (*see* page 65)
3 small potatoes

The night before you plan to eat, leave the haricot beans to soak.

On the cooking day, choose a deep lidded flameproof casserole and fill it with the water. Drop in the drained beans. Peel the onions and chop them in half lengthways, trimming off any whiskers, but leaving the root end intact, as this helps keep the halves together. Insert 1 clove into each half. They can go in the pot too. Tie up in a string the thyme sprigs with the bay leaves. In they go with a good grind of black pepper and grate of nutmeg. Peel the garlic cloves, split them in two and throw them in.

If using the bacon, remove the rind, but save it for larding or soups. Take the bacon or hock and gently lower it into the water. Bring it to the boil, skim with a ladle and turn it down to a simmer. Put on the lid, checking the temperature once more, as this will increase the heat within the pot. Cook this for 1$^3/_4$ hours, skimming occasionally.

Top and peel the carrots, turnips and swede, chopping them as you see fit (the pieces should be big). Trim and clean the leeks, and cut each in two or three. Have all these waiting in a bowl. Shred the cabbage into 5cm wide ribbons, including the core, and wash. Leave in the colander.

Take the confit duck legs and, having de-fatted and skinned them, split them in half. Have these ready next to the vegetables.

After 1 3/4 hours, put all the vegetables in with the bacon or ham. Peel the potatoes, rinse them and add them too. Replace the lid and bring back to a simmer. The introduction of the vegetables will mean you need to skim the broth again after about 10 minutes. Cook for half an hour. After 20 minutes, finally drop in all the duck pieces and cook for the last 10 minutes. When ready, the vegetables should all be soft but not collapsed.

When guests give signals of hunger, lift the bacon or hock from the broth to a board and carve it into thick slices. Put them in the middle of a large serving dish, surrounded by different coloured piles of each vegetable and duck confit. Check the seasoning of the broth. The ham and duck should salt it perfectly, but you may like a little more. Pour over a ladleful of the tasty broth, and set the dish in the middle of the table. Separately serve everyone a bowl of the broth on the side, not forgetting to fish out the beans at the bottom. Alternatively, serve everything up in shallow soup plates – broth, meats and vegetables all mixed up. Open a bottle of Bordeaux and sit it next to a large pot of French mustard, a warm country loaf and a large block of good butter. Life is good.

DUCK WITH WALNUT SAUCE

I came across this dish in France with my parents, in possibly the most hideously decked-out (in apricot) restaurant I have ever encountered. Truly alarming. We all got the giggles and didn't think anything good would come to the table. We were right, except for the following dish, which works well in this version using wild duck. Robust and earthy, this is something I only cook in the company of one other, a bottle of Armagnac and a plan to stay up talking all night. An extravagent little dish, it is worth the effort.

Serves 2

1 mallard, hung, plucked and cleaned, or
   1 small farmed duckling
2 tablespoons vegetable oil
1 medium onion, quartered and not peeled

900ml water
50g shelled walnuts
olive oil
large-flaked sea salt and black pepper
butter
2 tablespoons double cream (optional)
100ml brandy

Have the butcher take the breasts from the duck for you. Keep the legs, carcass and liver. Concerning the legs; either add them to the stock with the skin removed or keep them for confit as they can be very tough, even when hung. Clean the carcass of any excess fat and skin. Cut it into four large pieces and, having heated the oil, fry them in a saucepan with the quartered onion over a medium-high heat for about 15 minutes. Pour over the water so that it just covers the duck; if it does not your pan is too big. Bring this to the boil and skim off any debris or scum that has floated to the surface, then reduce the heat so that the stock simmers rapidly. Simmer like this for about 40 minutes; you should be left with half the liquid. (As the stock reduces, if you feel peckish this is a good time to fry the liver in a little butter and deglaze with a little sherry vinegar. Eat on a small round of buttered toast with a grind of pepper and salt. Chef's perk.)

Whizz the walnuts briefly in a blender, but do not turn them to dust. Put them aside.

Remove the stock from the heat and strain through a colander into a smaller clean saucepan. Throw the duck wreckage away. Add the walnuts to the stock and simmer for a further 15 minutes, until the stock is well reduced and the walnuts softened. Pass this all through a sieve into a bowl, really pressing the walnuts to get every scrap of their essence. Return the liquid to the washed pan.

With a sharp knife, score the duck breast skin in a criss-cross pattern before rubbing it all over with olive oil, salt and pepper.

Heat a generous knob of butter in a pan until the butter is just turning brown. Put all the duck breasts in, skin-side-down, with a couple of small plates on top to keep them firmly pressed down to the source of the heat. Fry them like this for about 4 minutes. Turn them over and do the same on the other side for about 3 minutes. If using duckling, add a further 2 minutes to each side. The breasts want to be pink inside or they will taste dry. Allow the meat to rest and relax.

Bring the walnut stock to the boil before reducing the heat slightly and adding the cream and brandy. Simmer for 3-4 minutes.

Carve the breasts into diagonal slices, holding the blade of the knife at an angle. Put a pool of your sauce into the centre of a warm plate, placing the duck, crisp-side up, in the middle. This eats tremendously well with the potato purée on page 191, or some peeled and halved apples that you have roasted with butter, sugar and a good splash of sherry vinegar. This is a good time for cider as well as white wine.

DUCK FAT ON TOAST

This can only be made using a homemade reserve of duck fat, as you will get the tasty jelly at the bottom and the flavour of any herbs you have used in the preserving of the duck.

Toast some good doughy brown bread and then spread a dollop of the duck fat on to the toast, getting a good amount of the brown jelly from the bottom of the container. Pepper heavily, finish with a bit of good salt and walk off, munching away.

DUCK WITH SAUERKRAUT

Don't pull a face at the thought of sauerkraut, instead walk to the shelf and pick up a jar. This treatment of cabbage is delicious and, when mixed with onions, apples, Riesling and bacon, a perfect nest is created for the duck, once more, to sit upon.

Fermenting cabbages at the perfect temperature, sauerkraut is a business of no light undertaking. It's one thing for me to ask you to marinate something a day in advance or cook something for 3 hours, but to have to fuss over a barrel of cabbage for 5 weeks is a business we will avoid. I think it better that you simply have this work done for you. With a large Polish community living in the UK, sauerkraut is found easily. Walk towards the things you might normally avoid; try sauerkraut.

With a large dollop of German mustard, this hearty eating should be saved for bitterly cold deep winter days. This recipe is an Alsatian treatment of sauerkraut.

Serves 4

1 large farmed duck (2.3kg)
large-flaked sea salt and black pepper
1 x 460g jar sauerkraut
1 tablespoon duck fat

1 large onion
200g smoked bacon lardons
8 juniper berries
2 bay leaves
2 apples, eg Cox
125ml Riesling white wine

Preheat the oven to 180°C/350°F/Gas 4.

Rinse the duck under the cold tap and, while wet, sprinkle it with 2 tablespoons of salt. Send it to the oven. Cook it for 1 hour at this temperature, basting it and pouring off the fat into your duck-fat container every 20 minutes. If you don't normally keep duck fat, start now.

Empty out the contents of the sauerkraut jar and flop it into a colander. Rinse it thoroughly under cold water and leave it to drain.

Melt the tablespoon of duck fat in a heavy pan on a medium heat. Skin, halve and slice the onion into thin slivers and add it to the pot with the lardons, juniper, bay leaves and a grinding of black pepper. This all wants to cook gently, the onion taking on no colour, for about 15 minutes. Peel the apples; they should be a firm and sweet variety with some sharpness – Cox's would do well here. Chop them into sugar-cube-sized squares before adding them to the pot, and cook for a further 5 minutes.

When the onions are soft, add the drained sauerkraut and the Riesling and mix all together well. Adjust the heat to gentle and cook this for about 15 minutes. Check it every now and then to make sure things are going to plan and that it is not catching or burning. The sauerkraut can sit on a very low heat until the duck is ready.

After an hour, turn the oven up to 220°C/425°F/Gas 7 in order to crisp up the duck. Do not use any fat after the temperature has been turned up, as it will burn. Cook for a further 15-20 minutes.

When done, take the duck out and let it stand for 5 minutes while you tend to the sauerkraut. Have a taste and adjust the seasoning should you need to. The duck skin is salted and, coupled with the smoked bacon, I wouldn't add any salt to the cabbage. But check.

Make a beautiful nest shape with the sauerkraut, with a shallow depression for the whole duck to sit in. Stick a carving fork straight into the top of the duck so that it stands upright and set the platter in the middle of the table. When all is carved, shared and served upon the plates, tuck in, not forgetting the large pot of sweet German mustard to smear on every forkful.

WOODCOCK

Under cold white skies, the woodcock slips into the British Isles when the weather is bitter and the frosted puddles are crisp. Mysterious in their look and silent jinking flight, they are but ghosts, invisible once settled on the leafy woodland floor in their bespoke tweedy camouflage. Seen on the move at dusk, their silent flight in silhouette is an eerie wonder. Resident woodcock may be seen all year round, their numbers being swelled by visitors from northern Europe here to enjoy the milder winters. However, it still needs to be cold and in warm winters there will be few. Because of this, some shoots prefer the woodcock left alone, as it's not every year they are now seen. This must be respected, but in a good cold winter I will take a few and cook them with reverence. The snipe is their tiny and equally delicious cousin who prefers the wetter ground of marshes, drains and bogs.

Order both these birds in advance because, due to weather conditions and the eagerness of hunters to keep them, they can be hard to obtain. Irritatingly, the price of woodcock varies between rural cheap to urban extortion. I have been asked to pay £35 a brace in London ('very hard to obtain, sir'), of course refusing and finding them out of town at £4.50 each.

On take-off, the woodcock and snipe empty their bowels in order to obtain a faster departure from the ground. Therefore, before roasting gutting is unnecessary, the innards also delivering those delicious, earthy, gamey dark unctions upon the toast. The meats of these birds are truly sensational and unforgettable once tasted. Traditionally, they are cooked with the head left on, the beak skewering one leg, but hey the tasty little brain is not for everyone. Roast woodcock on buttered toast in an oven preheated to 200°C/400°F/Gas 6 for approximately 15 minutes, splashing with some brandy.

GAMEBIRD TERRINE

Simply roasted, the woodcock can hardly be improved upon. However, this terrine was the result of a bored Sunday afternoon, a couple of regular inhabitants of an otherwise empty fridge and the spoils of a wet weekend's rough-shooting.

Serves 4-6

a brace of woodcock, pigeons or partridges
150g pork belly, without rind
30g butter
1 small Spanish onion, peeled and finely chopped
4 sage leaves, finely chopped
1 teaspoon caster sugar
1 tablespoon sherry
crushed heads of 4 cloves
a generous pinch of large-flaked sea salt and thorough grind of black pepper
a splash of milk
10 rashers of streaky dry-cured bacon, de-rinded if necessary

Preheat the oven to 180°C/350°F/Gas 4.

Skin the birds, cutting off all the meat and not wasting one iota (reserve the liver and heart, and, only if using woodcock, the intestines too). Chop the meat and the pork belly into small chunks. Put all this meat, including the offal, into a food processor and blend well. Put to one side in a mixing bowl.

Melt the butter in a small frying pan, then add the onion and sage. Cook the onion until totally soft, about 10 minutes. Introduce the sugar and sherry, and carry on cooking until the onion is golden brown and the sherry has been absorbed.

Add the onion, the crumbled heads of the cloves (not the tough stem bit) and seasoning to the minced meat, and mix together thoroughly. Add a small amount of milk just to loosen the mix a little. Put the frying pan back on the heat and fry a little pat of the mince, tasting when cooked and cooled to see if your seasoning is correct.

Take a medium pudding basin or a deep ovenproof bowl and line criss-cross-style with three big pieces of clingfilm so that a good amount hangs over the edge of the bowl. Then line the bowl with the bacon rashers all overlapping, with some hanging out round the edges. Spoon in the uncooked meat, making sure it's nicely packed down. Fold the bacon over the top before pulling the clingfilm over to close the top. Cut a small round lid from a cardboard box, wrap in clingfilm and place this on the clingfilm, with weights on top.

Boil the kettle and pour about 3cm water into a deep baking tray. Lower the filled bowl or pudding basin into the water. Put the whole setup into the preheated oven and cook for 45 minutes. After this time, take the terrine from the oven, remove the weights and slide a skewer or thin knife through the clingfilm into the middle of the meat. Leave it for 30 seconds. Remove the point and touch your lip with it: if it is warm, you have arrived; if cold, put the terrine back in the oven for another 10 minutes.

Discard the tray and water and let the terrine cool a bit before placing it in the fridge with the weights.

When ready to enter, undo the clingfilm, turn the terrine out on to a plate, pull all the clingfilm off and marvel at how artful your bacon outside looks. Eat the terrine with good bread or hot toast, lots of unsalted butter and some crunchy gherkins. Best eaten a day after it has been made.

WOOD PIGEON

Maybe the wood pigeon's 'coo-coo-coo-coo' heard from bed reminds you of the warm early mornings of summer, but in the autumn, as the harvest is gathered, they leave their leafy treetop cover and flutter to the stubble to banquet. This is a great time of year to hunt them. Here on the ground they will peck themselves stupid, getting so stuffed that take-off requires a good run, lots of flapping and considerable exertion. Some old poachers' stories will tell you that they can be chased, scooped up by hand and popped in a sack. I tried this, targeted the fattest pigeon, failed and felt like a complete turnip on realizing I was being watched from a passing tractor, one field away. On these evenings, though, with a gun and a strong position, I can gather a good few birds. The wood pigeon is otherwise very wily and will take to the wing at the slightest glimpse of the hunter, or faintest snap of a twig underfoot. The wood pigeon is a clean-living country bird and must not be confused with the grozzled wretches in our cities.

WARM SALAD OF PIGEON, ROAST CHICORY AND PICKLED WALNUTS

This salad is very tasty in all parts, making a crack team, as you will see. When in season, a carefully skinned and segmented blood orange (or orange) is a delicious addition to this dish. Mix it through with the leaves.

The roast chicory alone goes very well with all other meats and fish such as bass.

Serves 4

1 small handful each of oakleaf lettuce and frisée lettuce
2 pickled walnuts
a small handful of shelled hazelnuts or walnuts
breasts of 2 wood pigeons
large-flaked sea salt and black pepper
20g butter

$^3/_4$ tablespoon walnut or hazelnut oil
1 tablespoon sherry vinegar
1 teaspoon Dijon mustard

ROAST CHICORY
1 big chicory head
1 tablespoon sherry vinegar
30g butter
2 teaspoons caster sugar

Preheat the oven to full whack. Cut a piece of greaseproof paper to the size of a baking tray and lay it on.

Remove any outside damaged or browned leaves from the chicory. Do not cut off the stem at the bottom, as this holds the pieces together. Split the chicory in half lengthways. Cut each half in four lengthways and lay them on the papered tray. Splash with the sherry vinegar, thumb over the top of the bottle, on the exposed sides of the chicory and dot them generously with little knobs of the butter. Grind over salt and pepper and finally sprinkle the pieces with the caster sugar. Put them in the oven for their first 15 minutes.

Pull some good leaves from the oakleaf lettuce, and choose the more tender middle leaves from the frisée, but not masses of either. Although a salad, the idea is not to obscure the pigeon as if it were back in the tree. Wash the leaves, but treat the oakleaf carefully, as it is easily bruised and damaged. Drain and dry thoroughly.

Next, harpoon the pickled walnuts from the jar and slice them thinly from end to end. They may crumble a little bit, but no matter. Put them to one side.

Check the chicory after 15 minutes. If it has started to brown, turn it over in the melted butter and return it to the oven. If not, give it longer. You want the chicory to be well browned and very frazzled all over. Check the pieces and turn, returning them to the oven until this is done.

For the last 3-4 minutes, toast the shelled nuts in the oven. When this task is completed, turn the oven to low just to keep the chicory warm.

Pull the skin off the pigeon breasts. Season them well with salt and pepper. Put a small frying pan on the heat with the butter and heat it until it is smoking.

While the pan heats, in a bowl, mix a couple of capfuls of the walnut or hazelnut oil, a good splash of sherry vinegar, seasoning and the Dijon mustard together. Don't use too much walnut or hazelnut oil as it is strong and the lettuce is only to be lightly dressed. When blended, toss in the leaves and move them about until well covered.

Put the pigeon breasts in the smoking pan and, without fiddling, leave them to cook for 2 minutes before turning them to do the same on the other side. If the breasts arch up in defiance while frying, press them down with a fork to get the sides nice and brown. When cooked, take them out of the pan and rest them.

Take the chicory from the oven, remove from the pan, flicking off any excess butter, and mix it through the leaves. With an open and light clasp, gently divide the salad between both plates, the chicory poking through, and all looking buoyant, not flat. Angling a knife at 45 degrees, slice each pigeon breast crossways into four and artfully pop two slices of breast on each salad. Sprinkle over the slices of pickled walnut and the coarsely chopped toasted nuts, and eat it sharpish with maybe a glass of cold cider.

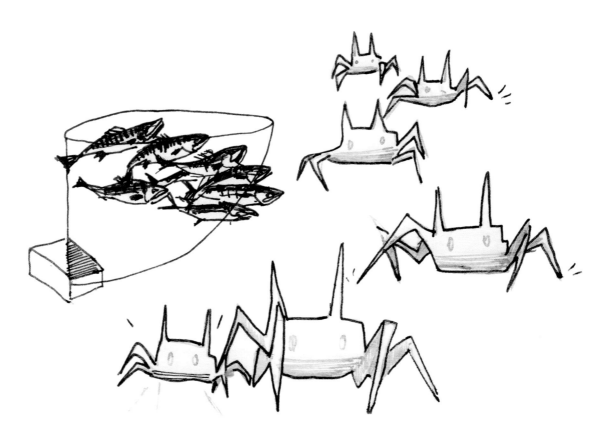

Val Werner

FISH DISHES

MACKEREL

If I were told that I could only eat one fish for the rest of my life, well then mackerel, with its permanent smirk, would win hands down. Spitting under the grill, pronged from vinegar, splashed with soy, I crave that rich, oily, mineral taste. They must be fresh, though; at their peak, stiff when held by the head. After that iridescent green fades to grey, they are not half the fish that lay quivering in the bucket or stared beadily from the crushed ice display. Buy mackerel when it's fresh and leave it when not.

Of course the best way to ensure quality is to catch them yourself. The best bait for mackerel is mackerel, a couple of 5cm-long skinny strips, preferably cut from the belly, on a No. 4 hook and a sliding polystyrene float set at about 8 feet and flung off the pier or beach. Use as light a spinning rod as possible (9 foot) for added fun. The best time is at sunset in September and October. If you keep on catching garfish, with only the occasional mackerel, slide the float 2 feet up the line and you will be in. This tends to be because the garfish, as they follow the mackerel, swim above them. Fly-fishing for mackerel is about as fun as it gets, but this is not a style that can be explained quickly, requiring a booklet of its own. These fish are easy to catch, so know when to stop, as the thrill can override the need.

MACKEREL IN OATS WITH WATERCRESS

Mackerel in this clothing is very delicious and one of my favourite lunches. I cannot recall ever eating this at dinner.

Have your fish filleted by the fishmonger. You will find that, as autumn fades into winter, the mackerel are getting much larger. So if you buy one of these huge Channel mackerel, a single fish will feed two people even for those as greedy as me.

Serves 2

1 large mackerel, filleted
1 medium egg
large-flaked sea salt and black pepper

1 big handful of medium porridge oats
butter
2 fistfuls of watercress, washed
juice of 1 lemon
Dijon mustard

Rinse the fish fillets and pat them dry with some kitchen paper. Break the egg into a bowl and whisk with a tiny dribble of tap water and some salt and pepper. Spread the oats on a plate.

Heat a big fat knob of butter in a frying pan on a medium heat. When the butter is foaming, take a fillet and introduce both sides to the egg wash before rolling it in the oats. Lay it to cook in the butter. Repeat the stages with the other fillet. Turn the fillets when golden brown and cook the other side. This will take about 3 minutes per side. If the fillets arch up in the middle, it might be worth resting a small plate on them to keep the skin and oats against the pan, ensuring crispiness.

While the fish is cooking, mix your watercress in a little bowl with some lemon juice and salt. Take a handful of the watercress to the plate and add a fried mackerel fillet to the side of it, *not on top*. A generous teaspoon of Dijon mustard will finish it off perfectly.

MACKEREL WITH GRATED TURNIPS AND GINGER

During my short-lived foray into the art world, I would take lunch in a little downstairs Japanese restaurant on the Tottenham Court Road. I never tired of the fish lunch there, eating it maybe three times a week while flicking through Manga comics. The simple and clean tastes left me feeling light, and the essential omega fishy oils equipped my brain with the renewed ability to decipher unintelligible art speak.

The mackerel can be replaced with horse mackerel, mullet or bass.

Serves 1

1 mackerel, gutted
good Japanese soy sauce

vegetable oil
1 fat thumb of fresh root ginger
1 medium turnip
Japanese sour plum pickles (if available)

Turn your grill on to full blast. Make sure the fish has been cleaned properly and is washed and then dried well.

Make shallow slits into the flesh of the fish on each side, rubbing with a little of the soy afterwards. (I really would stress here that the Japanese table soy tastes less yeasty and is a better option than the Chinese styles of soy, which can be a bit Marmitey.) Take a shallow oven tray and rub a bit of vegetable oil the same size as the fish on the bottom. Lay the fish on the tray and pop it under the grill, high enough to be quite close to the heat, but not touching it.

In the meantime, skin the ginger and grate it on the setting in between the one you can never pick anything out of and the one you do kids' Cheddar on. Take a plate and put the little mound of ginger on it. Next, skin and grate the turnip as you have the ginger. Squeeze out some of the water and then make it into a little mountain next to the ginger.

The mackerel will need about 4-5 minutes on each side; allow for the extra minute if the mackerel is really large. As the mackerel cooks, each side will take on a beautiful golden hue. The oil you put on the tray should allow you to turn the fish without it sticking, as will the fish's natural oils.

When your mackerel is done, lift it on to the plate with the ginger and turnip. Take to the table with chopsticks, accompanied by a small saucer of pickles (no matter if you have none, as they are not essential). Pour some soy into the turnip mound and eat the fish with this and a nip of ginger. Drink with a good mug of hot green tea.

PICKLED MACKEREL

I am a huge fan of pickled and cured fish, with one of my fridge-door shelves the territory of kippers, rollmops and pickled mackerel only. Without them close by, I feel unsettled and nervous.

If one has become a little over-enthusiastic on a successful mackerel haul, then this is an excellent way to deal with the glut. I lean more towards a sweeter pickling than a sour one. This method is incredibly easy, and the end result is very satisfying to look upon. When pickling, you are thinking ahead and preserving your future. Leave the fish unopened for at least three days after you have made it. A week would improve things even more. Pick the freshest mackerel you can find. Remember that you want that green-blue iridescent fish, not that rainy-day grey colour

If multiplying the measurements, I advise dividing this recipe among small jars, as this reduces the possibility of waste through peckishness.

Fills 1 x 500ml jar

2 medium mackerel, filleted
4 level tablespoons large-flaked sea salt
4 level tablespoons unbleached white
    sugar

1 small red onion
red wine vinegar
6 bay leaves
10 juniper berries
1 level teaspoon fennel seeds
10 black peppercorns

Fillet the mackerel if it has not been done already; it is important to make sure that the ribs are removed. Before pickling, rinse the fillets briefly and pat them dry with some kitchen paper. Take out the pin bones with tweezers. (These are the little upright bones that travel slightly beyond halfway down the centre of each fillet, from behind the head. It is a little fiddly, but you will soon get the hang of it. Feel for them by running your fingertip just above the middle of each fillet from the head end – you will feel their tips sticking out of the flesh.) Pull them out in order, one by one; they will come quite easily. Don't go jabbing and gouging at this job, or you will make a real mess of your mackerel fillet. Do it with the precision of a great 1920s beauty plucking her eyebrows.

Lay the fillets, skin-side down and side by side, on a plate before mixing together the salt and half the sugar. Scatter this evenly over all the fillets and then gently rub it into the fish. Leave them to one side, covered, in a cool place for an hour.

Peel, halve and thinly slice the onion. Bring a small pan of water to the boil and briefly drop in the onion slivers for approximately 10 seconds to soften them. Drain them thoroughly. Mix 300ml of the vinegar with the remaining sugar and stir until the sugar has dissolved.

Rinse the fillets briefly under a cold tap and pat them dry. Slice them from head to tail in 3cm slices. Leave the tail end a little longer in length. Layering the fish alternately with slivers of onion, bay and spices, fill the inside of a 500ml sterilized airtight jar. Pour over the vinegar solution and top up, if need be, with extra unsweetened vinegar until it is close to the rim of the jar. Seal the jar tightly with a lid and refrigerate.

Dangling my legs over a rocky ledge or pier and watching my float for any knocks, I load rough rips of bread with the pickled mackerel. The mackerel will store well for about 3 weeks in the fridge, but should be eaten within a few days once opened.

MACKEREL ON TOAST WITH SALTED CUCUMBER AND HORSERADISH

There are a few parts to this, but all are very easy.

Serves 1

1 medium mackerel, filleted
large-flaked sea salt and black pepper
butter

SALTED CUCUMBER AND HORSERADISH
¹/₂ cucumber
1 tablespoon large-flaked sea salt

some fresh horseradish
1 heaped tablespoon crème fraîche
1 teaspoon English mustard powder

TO SERVE
1 slice of soda bread (*see* page 236)
1 small red onion
butter
¹/₂ small lemon

Skin the cucumber and slice on a grater on the single-blade side or on a mandoline. If you are chopping the slices, they must be cut very thin. Put the slices in a sieve or colander and throw in enough salt to make you think you have added a little too much. This is correct. Mix in the salt well and leave the contents to drip over the sink for half an hour. Then quickly run a little cold water over the cucumber and let it drain. Pick the pieces up and wring them out, your close-cupped hands shaking with exertion to expel any last drips. When you have got as much water out as you can, leave them to one side. Their texture has now changed to a wonderful collapsed yet bitey consistency.

Next, skin and finely grate enough horseradish to really blast the nostrils when eating, about a half-clenched fistful. In a bowl, mix this with the crème fraîche and mustard powder, making sure the powder is properly mixed in, with no lumps. Leave to one side when done.

Cut a slice of soda bread and sit it in the toaster, but don't send it down. Thinly slice the small red onion and put to one side.

Give your mackerel fillets a quick rinse and a wipe with some kitchen paper. Salt and pepper the mackerel fillets on their skin side. Heat a good knob of butter in a frying pan until it is foaming and add the fillets, skin-side down. Place one side-plate over both the fillets, as this will make sure they cook flat and evenly and that the skin will be nice and browned.

Send down the toast. The fish will be done after about 4 minutes, when, on lifting the plate, you see only a pale translucent pink in the middle of the fish fillet the width and breadth of your little finger. Turn off the heat.

The toast being done, butter it well and put it on a plate. Lay a small handful of cucumber on the toast. Flip the fillets over in the cooling frying pan for 5 seconds, then put side by side on top of the cucumber. Place a good dollop of the horseradish sauce on top. Finish with slivers of the red onion and a squeeze of lemon. Tuck in! Don't faff, this needs eating immediately.

GREY MULLET

Unfortunately for the grey mullet, its reputation for mooning around in harbours visible just under spluttering boats and floating petrol slicks leaves few with any desire to lift a forkful towards the mouth. However, this is one of my favourite fish and I would, you might think rashly, state that I consider it as good as the sea bass. What's more, it is gratifyingly cheap, which prompts others to again think it inferior. If taken from clean waters they are delicious.

Notoriously wary of the hook and easily spooked, don't take the grey mullet's wandering laid-back appearance for granted. One false move and in a flash they're gone. I have heard of them caught with chocolates (obviously not coffee creams) and bits of red thread, but the following method is one I heard of in a pub in Ireland and find particularly intriguing.

Bait their swim two days before you plan your attack with cheap pulpy bread. This will keep the mullet in the area. On fishing day, pick sheep's wool from a barbed-wire fence and wind it round a teeny fly hook to imitate a small piece of white bread. Throw more bread to the mullet before casting your fly between the bobbing crusts. Hopefully the mullet, fooled, will sip it down and you're off. You cannot bully these fish to the net, so be careful, for fighting a 7lb mullet has been likened to hooking a passing moped.

GREY MULLET WITH CHARMOULA

Oh, this is so easy and the results are fabulous. This treatment of fish is Moroccan. The herbs are changeable, but normally consist of various combinations of mint, parsley and coriander. I was not aware that it could ever be made with only parsley until ordering it in the seedy harbour of Tangier. It was cooked by a thuggish proprietor called Popeye who more resembled Bluto, his arms were so thick, but his fish dishes were excellent. The bunches of parsley should not be those little supermarket tufts, but a big flower-bunch size. Either halve the recipe for a smaller fish or make the full amount, as charmoula is great to eat as a salad.

Serves 6

1 x 2kg grey mullet, gutted, scaled
   and fins removed
olive oil

CHARMOULA
2 big bunches of fresh parsley

2 medium red onions
2 good hard garlic cloves
2 good fat ripe tomatoes
1 tablespoon cumin seeds
2 teaspoons cayenne pepper
125ml olive oil
juice of 1 lemon
large-flaked sea salt

Preheat the oven to 220°C/425°F/Gas 7.

Wash the mullet once more and wipe it down with kitchen paper. Make four cuts, evenly spaced, from head to tail. Cut into where the flesh is deepest, along the back of the fish; cutting into shallow ribs will not aid the cooking.

Pick all the leaves from the parsley, wash them and make sure they are dried thoroughly in a salad spinner or on a tea towel. Chop the parsley to medium-fine and put it into a large mixing bowl. Peel and chop the onions to the finest dice you can and add these to the bowl as well. Do the same with the garlic.

Put the kettle on and get some water boiling. Cut the stem out of the tomatoes with a small knife and cut a shallow cross on the bottom. Put them in a heatproof bowl and cover them with boiling water. Count to 30 before tipping the water away. Peel the tomatoes and take out the seeds. Chop them roughly to the size of a five-pence piece with straight sides. (Sorry, I couldn't think of better terminology). Add them to the bowl. Toast the cumin seeds in a dry pan, but do not burn them. Yes, in the bowl they go. Finally, add 1 heaped teaspoon of the cayenne pepper, the olive oil and the lemon juice to the bowl. Season with salt to taste, although I advocate one more pinch on top of what you think is right. Mix everything up thoroughly.

Take two long sheets of foil, long enough so that when each is doubled over they're about 8cm longer than the fish at both ends. Doubling over the foil should prevent the bag from ripping. Lay one doubled sheet on the work surface and oil the area the fish will sit on, making sure that you really have covered the tail and head ends, as they can get gluey and stick to the foil, resulting in damage to the mullet when turned out. Salt the oiled area lightly. Put the fish on the foil. Opening up the belly cavity with one hand, pack all the charmoula into the fish, including the now-empty gill area. Pour any juice around the fish. Oil the fish on the upside and sprinkle with a little more salt. Take the top sheet of foil and lay it over the fish. Work all the way round the two sheets, folding the edges over and inwards about three times and leaving a small baggy area between the folded edges and the mullet.

Gently lay your shiny parcel in the preheated oven. It will take longer than you think to cook; I would suggest about an hour. Before you even think of checking the fish, the loose area of the bag should have puffed up with steam. To check the fish is cooked, take a thin knife and push the tip in just behind the head. This is where the flesh is deepest. It should slide in easily, with only the faintest resistance as the knife approaches the backbone.

When the time has passed, take the fish from the oven and put the bag on a suitable serving dish, one with sides, as you will find a lot of tasty juice within. Unwrap the bag, being careful not to let your hands get caught by the steam. If you feel you can slide fishy from the foil on to the plate, do so, otherwise serve it from the open foil. Make sure everyone gets some of the fish and stuffing along with some juice. It goes well served with steamed couscous.

A FISH SOUP OF MULLET

This stew is a robust dish with plenty of attitude, a beautiful colour and a faint back-of-throat burn from the chilli. It is so easy to prepare, but there's no need to let on unless asked. Don't be mean with the saffron: it requires a good pinch for that wonderful hint of iodine taste. Saffron being important in this dish, try to use the real McCoy (ideally in little perspex boxes tied with glinting string), as minced flower-petal trimmings peddled by tricksters in holiday markets are time-wasting nonsense and will add no joy to your stew.

Serves 6

olive oil
1 garlic bulb
1 teaspoon coriander seeds
2 fresh bay leaves
1 pinch of dried oregano
1 Spanish dried guanjillo chilli,
     or other dried medium-hot chilli
2 small onions, peeled and finely sliced

5 tomatoes, peeled and deseeded
300ml dry white wine
a generous pinch of saffron strands
1 teaspoon tomato purée
juice of 1 orange
5 medium waxy potatoes
large-flaked sea salt and black pepper
1 x 1.5kg mullet, filleted and skinned
chopped parsley
extra virgin olive oil

Heat a really good slug of olive oil – and I mean a really good slug – in a wide, shallow lidded saucepan. If you do not have one, a lidded flameproof casserole is fine.

Split the garlic bulb from side to side across the middle and place the halves, cut-side down, in the oil. Let them slowly sizzle, on not too fierce a heat, to a dark golden colour. Don't worry about the garlic skins; they can be pushed to the side when eating the stew. Chuck in the coriander seeds, bay, oregano, whole chilli and onions. Sweat until the onions are soft but not coloured. Chop the tomatoes. Add the wine, saffron, tomatoes, tomato purée and orange juice, and cook for a further 10 minutes on a slow simmer.

While this cooks, peel and halve the potatoes lengthways, cutting each half into six pieces. Rinse them and add them to the stew, making sure they are all submerged in the sauce. Add a little extra water if need be, about 150ml, with a good teaspoon of salt. Cook, with the lid on, on a gentle simmer until nearly done, about 10-12 minutes.

While the potatoes cook, cut the mullet fillets into large mouthfuls. When the potatoes are done, add the fish pieces, making sure they are sitting in the soup, not on top of it. Return the lid, and cook for a little more than 6 minutes. Don't forget, you can always take out a piece of fish and taste it. Taste for seasoning as well.

Serve this rich stew in bowls sprinkled with chopped parsley and with a dash of extra virgin olive oil on top.

CONGER EEL

I feel strangely attached to the conger eel: sorry for it in the aquarium sulking in a broken chimney pot, and reverent of the big line-breaking brutes lurking in the inky black wrecks 50,000 leagues under the sea. Although many people are put off by the conger's faded appearance, the meat has a surprisingly firm and delicious flesh, which is not greasy, unlike some other types of eel. The meat also allows for a little overcooking if accidentally ignored, as it does not seem to dry out or fall apart. This, however, is not an excuse for sloppiness. When crispy banknotes are few and short change prevalent, it is a cheap and tasty option.

POT-ROAST EEL WITH JERUSALEM ARTICHOKES

This is a very humble little recipe, but delivers a very tasty dish. The sweetness of Jerusalem artichoke goes really well with fish.

Serves 2

300g conger fillet
black pepper
4 rashers of smoked streaky bacon
1 medium onion

1 bay leaf
1 tablespoon malt vinegar
3 medium Jerusalem artichokes
30g butter
large-flaked sea salt

Preheat the oven to 200°C/400°F/Gas 6.

The ideal pot for this dish would be a small earthenware crock or otherwise heavy casserole, one in which the ingredients are not crammed but fitted snugly.

Wash the conger fillet, patting it dry with a good amount of kitchen paper. Grind black pepper all about it, but you don't need any salt at this stage. Wrap the bacon rashers round the conger eel, not worrying if they do not go all the way around. You should end up with a nice stripy, Brighton rock appearance.

Peel the onion and slice it into very fine slivers. If they are too thick, they will not cook to soft in the time they are intended to.

Put the bay leaf in the bottom of the pot with the onions scattered on top. Splash them about with the vinegar. Peel and split the Jerusalem artichokes lengthways in six and lay them around the inside edge of the pot. Dot the butter all about the onions and artichokes, saving a little knob to pop on top of the eel. Season them both with some salt and more black pepper.

Lower the conger eel into the middle of its seat and add the last bit of butter. Put the lid on and roast the eel for **30-35** minutes in the preheated oven. When the lid is removed, the conger should be sitting in its fabulous juices surrounded by the softened onions and Jerusalem artichokes.

Simplicity itself. Eat with warm crusty bread and a bottle of good cider.

OTHER AUTUMN FISH

CRISPY GURNARD AND SPLIT PEAS

Staring deep into the eyes of a gurnard sitting on shelf two of my fridge, I'm having a telepathic encounter. 'Yes, you're right,' I say, 'you and mushy peas it is!'

Three species of gurnard live in British waters: the tub, red and silver gurnard. The gurnard is an extraordinary looking creature. Picking its way over the seabed, it hunts with its long spindly fingers, set beneath its pectoral fins, manoeuvring them like a pianist in the sand and silt. Little critters disturbed by this 'grabbly' raking foolishly dash from their cover only to disappear forever into the armoured box head of the gurnard. When brought into the boat, this indignant fish will often insist on being returned to the water with a series of surprising croaks. Silent ones go into the bucket, croakers go back.

This fish does really well in crispy batter. I love radioactive-green marrowfat peas, but dried split peas are just as good.

Serves 2

2 x 250g gurnard fillets or a collection of smaller ones
large-flaked sea salt and black pepper
vegetable oil, for deep-frying
1 lemon, halved
malt vinegar

MUSHY PEAS
1 medium onion, peeled

200g dried peas, soaked overnight
2 bay leaves
2 litres water
a generous knob of butter
a splash of malt vinegar

BATTER
200g plain flour
30g dried yeast
1 x 330ml bottle lager

Put the onion in a pan with the drained soaked peas and bay leaves. Cover with the water and put on a slow simmer, uncovered, for at least 2 1/2 hours. Check mid-cooking to make sure they are not drying out, as one man's simmering is another man's boiling.

After 2 hours, turn your attention to the batter, which will need to stand for about 40 minutes before use. Sift the flour into a bowl, and stir in the yeast and a pinch of salt. Pour in the lager and whisk as you go. Leave to one side. After a while, you will notice a bubbling and fizzing taking place. This is good.

The peas should be very soft with no resistance to the bite. It might seem logical at this point to throw away the water the peas are in. Don't!

Keep enough that it lies just below the level of the peas, blitzing it up with the peas and the butter in a processor or blender until it is as smooth as it will go. If the peas are still a little liquid, return them to the heat and bring them down to the consistency of mushy peas, which I am sure you have seen before. If you have to do this, put an upside-down colander or sieve over the top of the pan, as they can burp and splutter all over the hob.

Now the peas are done, add the salt. A teaspoon should do it, but they may take a little more. Add a splash of vinegar, about $^1/_2$ capful. Put to one side to heat up again when your fish is ready.

Bring your fryer or pan of oil to between 180 and 190°C/350-375°F. Test that the temperature is correct by dropping a small piece of batter into the oil, which should skate madly about the surface. You are ready to lower the fish in.

Pat the gurnard fillets dry. If you take a wet fish to batter, as you drag the fillet through the batter it will slide off. Give the fish a little seasoning (this will also help to keep the batter where it should be). Before introducing the fish to the batter, bang the base of the bowl against the table top to knock out a few of the bubbles, as, when large, they are too fragile and will crack or pop when fried, letting in the oil; this is not good.

After dunking the fish, dangle it over the bowl to make sure any excess drips off. Take it to its hot bath. The timing here is visual. The fish wants to be deep golden on both sides, which won't take very long, about 4-6 minutes to cook the whole fillet, depending on its size. If in doubt, go for a darker colour, as pale, undercooked batter is not fun. Remember when frying without a thermostatically controlled fryer to be very alert and calm. Remove the fish to some waiting kitchen paper to drain.

To serve, make a lovely mound of piping hot peas in the middle of the plate and lay your crispy gurnard on top, serving with a lemon half, a sprinkling of malt vinegar and salt. If you are a neurotic, serve the peas on the side in a ramekin. Sorry, I haven't included chips; I only ever eat my fish with mushy peas, odd bod that I am.

BAKED SOLE WITH BROWN SHRIMPS AND CELERY LEAVES

In the interest of sales, witch sole is now unromantically called Torbay sole. Although I understand this change of name, I enjoy the fairy-tale connotations of this fish climbing on to craggy rocks at night and transforming into a hag or a young maiden to lure ships and sailors to their end, once more becoming a helpless flatty at dawn. Therefore bake witches. They are delicious and reasonably priced, with a delicate texture lying somewhere between lemon and Dover sole, which also work well here.

I'm very greedy with fish, so the following recipe serves one.

Serves 1

1 x 450g sole, ideally witch, gutted
2 tablespoons plain flour

large-flaked salt and black pepper
25g butter
1 handful of brown shrimps
a small handful of celery leaves
$^1/_2$ lemon

With sole, look for a fish with a lot of slime and clear eyes: the more slime, the fresher the fish.

Preheat the oven to 220°C/425°F/Gas 7.

Using a table knife, scrape against the direction of the scales, under running water. Do this on both sides. Pick the sole up in one hand and cut away the fins round both sides of the body. Do the same with the tail, and sadly, if you cannot fit the whole fish in your largest frying pan, cut the head off too. I always prefer to see fish cooked whole.

Sift the flour on to a plate and grind in a very generous amount of salt. Take an ovenproof non-stick frying pan or baking tray big enough for your fish and put it on the heat. Add 10g of the butter and melt it.

When the butter starts foaming, wipe the fish with kitchen paper and place it in the flour, turning it on to the other side and spanking off any excess with your hand. Place the sole, dark-side down, in the pan and fry it for about 2 minutes, not disturbing it. After this time, flip it over on to its white side and dot the top with the remaining butter. Put the whole fish in the preheated oven and cook for about 5 minutes. Add the brown shrimps and return the fish to the oven for another 2 minutes. Test for doneness by putting a knife tip in behind where the head is (or was). It should slide in, touching the bone, but with the faintest resistance.

When left to my own devices, I like to eat the fish straight from the pan. Finely chop the celery leaves and scatter them about the fish. Cut a wedge of lemon and squeeze this all over too. Sit down to the frying pan (why muck about with plates?) and deconstruct the witch, savouring its magical, subtle taste, making sure that a few shrimps and a bit of leaf hop on board each bite.

SALMON, LEEK AND POTATO SOUP

Fish heads often end up in the bin, resulting in a tasty meal carelessly disregarded. Extra satisfaction lies in the knowledge that fishy was shown its deserved respect. Salmon heads are cheap, providing a dinner that would make the meanest scrimper smile. I'm including this as autumn/winter cooking as I freeze the heads of any salmon I've decided to keep after using the body – for gravadlax or smoking.

Serves 2-4

2 salmon heads, eyes removed
1 teaspoon celery salt
2 bay leaves
a knob of butter

2 leeks, washed and chopped
a pinch of freshly grated nutmeg
a heavy grind of black pepper
2 medium potatoes
a dash of hot chilli sauce
2 tablespoons chopped fresh parsley

Clean the heads under cold running water, pulling out all the gills and picking out any clots of blood. This is important, because if not removed they will turn the broth bitter. Place the heads in a suitable pan, just covering them with cold water. Add the celery salt and bay leaves. Bring to a low simmer and cook for 15 minutes. Turn off the heat, remove the heads to a plate and allow them to cool.

Strain the broth of scales and bits into a bowl. Clean the pan and return to a medium heat, adding the butter, leeks, nutmeg and pepper. While the leeks cook, peel and dice the potatoes, rinsing them thoroughly to wash off excess starch. Add the potatoes to the leeks and pour over the broth, simmering until cooked, about 10 minutes.

While the vegetables cook, pick all the meat off the fish heads, taking special care not to overlook hidden succulent morsels.

When the potatoes are soft, after about 15 minutes, add the salmon pieces and cook for a further minute. Serve immediately in a bowl with a dash of hot chilli sauce and a little chopped parsley. Eat with hot toast smeared in butter and anchovy paste.

GRILLED SALMON HEADS: *Clean under cold water as in the recipe above, then split lengthways between the eyes and given a good grilling on both sides, the heads are delicious picked over with chopsticks and dipped in a little Japanese soy sauce. Eat with two small piles alongside, one of finely grated ginger, the other of grated turnip.*

SIGNAL CRAYFISH

We can no longer feast upon the sweet meats of our polite and timid little native northern white-clawed crayfish, for they are now protected. Fat, garish, destructive, obviously American, our rivers are overrun with the signal crayfish, identifiable by its plum-coloured body, blue under-claw (hence its name) and large size. How have we let this happen? During the 1970s, in an attempt to expand crayfish production into a commercial industry, the signal was introduced, favoured for its plumpness and fast growth. It arrived with a virus that our own crayfish were not equipped to repel. Either dying of this plague (which the invaders are immune to) or being left homeless and hungry, our native crayfish, with heads bowed, would shuffle off. Today they have few places left beyond the claws of their adversaries. As a result they are now protected. Meanwhile, the signal marches on, undermining the riverbanks with its burrowing and guzzling everything in its path.

In turn, it is your earthbound duty to guzzle as many of these imposters as you can. Our rivers (chalk-beds only due to the calcium crayfish need to grow their shells) are teeming with signal crayfish. With the help of a trap sunk with fresh fish inside, an unending source of sweet mouthfuls are at hand. In order that you may sit beside a bowl of mayonnaise surrounded by broken red shells, you must first obtain a licence. This ensures that should you trap one of our white-clawed countrymen you'll recognize it and pop it back. I have one thing to say of the signal crayfish – *melt butter and declare war*.

CRAYFISH WITH HAZELNUT AND PASTIS BUTTER

I could eat these stuffed crayfish from dawn till dusk. Select the larger ones if you can, as they will give you a better meat-to-stuffing ratio. If you have trapped them, don't put the small ones back, just eat them with mayonnaise later. This recipe requires live crayfish that must be dispatched. If you are the squeamish type, I wouldn't read beyond this point.

A crayfish sitting is a messy business, worthy of tucking a napkin into the collar of your shirt and using your fingers. This recipe works well with langoustines and would feed five.

Serves 2-4

30 signal crayfish
lemon wedges, to serve

STUFFING
a large handful of shelled hazelnuts
1 lemon

a large handful of picked parsley leaves
1 big ripped handful of slightly stale,
    good rustic bread
125g butter, cut into small cubes
2 good garlic cloves, peeled
a good splash of pastis
large-flaked sea salt and a big grind of
    black pepper

Turn the oven to its grill setting.

Grate the lemon zest on the medium-fine holes. Wash the parsley leaves, drying them thoroughly. Chop by hand as finely as you can. In a food processor, break the stale bread into medium-fine crumbs, not dust. Add all the remaining stuffing ingredients, except for the parsley, to the breadcrumbs and blend until thoroughly combined. If it forms into a lump, remove the lid and break it up a little with a spoon. When all is blended well, add the parsley and blend once more. Don't try to chop the parsley in the processor, as it will take on a chlorophyll taste. Not nice! Once chopped with a knife, when put in the blender the blades will not be able to chop it further.

Take each crayfish, holding it behind the front claws, at the armpits so to speak. It cannot nip you when held in this way. Hold it down on the table and put the tip of a long, sharp knife into the centre of its head. Push = crunch = dead. This manoeuvre will kill the crayfish instantly. Pick it up, holding the tail end. In the centre of the actual tail, take the middle piece and gently twist it between your thumb and forefinger. Pull away as you twist and the signal's waste sac should come out attached to the tailpiece. If it does not go according to plan, don't worry, they can be picked out with the tip of a knife once the crayfish have been split in half. Cut all the crayfish lengthways from tip to tail using the point you made in the head to start. When this is done, remove any waste sacs you did not previously remove.

Take an oven tray, your stuffing and a knife, and set them down next to the crayfish. Pick up a generous amount of the stuffing and paste it on the flesh side of each half crayfish. You really want a good teaspoon's worth per half. Lay them, side by side, on the tray as you prepare them. When all are done, sprinkle them all over with salt and put the tray beneath the grill. They will want to cook relatively close to the actual grill for about 4 minutes. They do not take long. The shells will go totally red, and if there is any remaining signs of dark brown or blue colouring, they are not ready and require a couple of minutes more.

When done, transfer them to a plate, stacking them up in rows, and serve with little lemon wedges. I think the red shells oozing with green butter look great. I like to accompany this with a cold pastis with ice and water.

LEFTOVERS: *This butter will freeze well and when needed is a fine application to a rack of lamb or grilled chicken.*

BOILED CRAYFISH WITH MAYONNAISE

I am from the school of peeling all my crayfish first, holding back the pleasure, before piling them all on to two pieces of bread with tons of mayo and butter, and eating them with the messy bit behind me.

For a mayonnaise to use in rémoulade, add more mustard and the sugar (*see* page 190). If you want garlic mayo, simply add three crushed garlic cloves at the beginning.

Serves 2-4

30 crayfish
lemon wedges
good bread and butter

MAYONNAISE
3 medium egg yolks

$1^1/_2$ heaped teaspoons Dijon mustard
2 teaspoons large-flaked sea salt
black pepper
juice of 1 lemon
50ml olive oil
250ml vegetable oil
a dash of hot water (about 20ml)

Dispatch the crayfish in the same way as described in the previous recipe, using the same manoeuvre to remove the waste sacs (if they don't come out, don't worry as they're harmless to eat). Making sure the water is boiling properly, boil them for 3 minutes before removing and allowing to cool.

When making mayonnaise, I find the sole use of olive oil can turn it somewhat bitter. This is why I have used only a little olive oil to a majority of vegetable oil. There are many myths about the making of mayonnaise: the cycles of the moon, the heat of the day, one's mood. This is nonsense. There is no mystery in it at all. Before relating the following recipe, I see absolutely no harm in quietly spooning 4 large tablespoons shop-bought mayo into a bowl and beating in a raw egg yolk, some Dijon mustard and a squeeze of lemon juice. No-one will know.

But if we want the real thing, then here goes. For the purposes of ease, we'll make it in the food processor, but should you be making it by hand, the order is the same, but vigorous beating will be needed – and possibly an extra person to hold the bowl down or pour the oil.

Put the egg yolks and mustard, salt, pepper and lemon juice in the bottom of the food processor. Turn on the blades and slowly, in a thin, thin stream, pour in the oil. If you find it has become too thick, and there is still oil to add, just add a tablespoon of warm water before continuing with the oil. If for some reason your mayo splits, do not throw it away, but start again with 1 egg yolk and $^1/_2$ teaspoon mustard before incorporating back in the disaster you created before.

Put the mayo in a tasteful bowl, and get cracking.

MUSSELS

I first recall eating mussels at the age of six – the boggling vision of a blue mountain was plonked into my low field of vision, casting a shadow over where I sat. Close-up hands tucked a napkin about my neck and gestured as to how I might use the empty pincer-like shell of one to tweezer out the meat of the others. Heaven! The same cannot be said for the family holidaying with us; their peace shattered by my fierce tantrums on being repeatedly told it was unreasonable for any child to have six bowls of *moules marinières* a day.

I love cooking with mussels, not only because of their wonderful sweet plumpness, but also because they are so versatile, being enjoyed with meat, in salads, soups and, as you will find, in generously stuffed empanadas. A slightly underdone mussel is infinitely better than an overcooked one, even though this may mean discarding one or two more than normal that may not have opened. In the UK mussels sold commerially must be purified under UV light for 42 hours. If you are harvesting them yourself for cooking, make sure you know how far away any sewerage outlets or pipes are. Try and avoid dredged mussels, as their collection vandalizes the sea floor.

MUSSEL EMPANADAS

Behind London's Blackfriars Road there is a little Chilean café called El Vergel. It is easily missed were it not for the happy queue of clientele waiting their turn to lunch on delicious things made by the smiling staff inside. But there is one thing I now find impossible not to order every time I go. It is nothing short of outstanding and totally worth a trip across town. The owners are so nice that I'm sure if I asked them for the recipe they would give it to me. But I don't feel I can. Here is my version.

Makes 5 empanadas

1kg mussels
2 medium onions
2 good garlic cloves
30g butter
1 teaspoon good saffron strands
1 level teaspoon ground cumin
2 medium eggs
1 good handful of picked parsley leaves

large-flaked sea salt and black pepper
vegetable oil, for shallow- to deep-frying

PASTRY
400g plain flour
2 teaspoons large-flaked sea salt
80g butter
200ml warm water
1 medium egg

Clean and de-beard the mussels (*see* page 117). Discard any that remain open if tapped. Put them to one side. Peel and finely chop the onions and garlic.

In a pan big enough to fit all the mussels, melt the butter over a medium heat. Add the onions and garlic, cooking them until totally soft but not coloured, about 10 minutes. When they are done, add the mussels, put the lid on the pan and cook for 3-4 minutes. You want the mussels to be just done and very soft. Remove the mussels, making sure as much of their juice remains in the pan as possible. Discard any that fail to open. Stir in the saffron and the cumin, leaving the juices gently simmering over the heat.

Put the mussels to cool. In another pan, hard-boil one of the eggs for 7 minutes before allowing it to cool as well.

Pick out all the mussel meat and discard the shells. Reduce the mussel juice by half, take it off the heat and allow it to cool also.

Roughly chop the mussel meat, and put it in a bowl before grating in the hard-boiled egg on the largest hole setting. Pick, wash, dry and roughly chop the parsley, adding this to the mussel stuffing. Mix in the remaining raw egg yolk. Give the stuffing a good grind of black pepper and about 1 teaspoon salt. Mix everything well before covering the bowl and leaving it in the fridge.

To make the pastry, sift the flour into a large mixing bowl and add the salt. Chop the butter, which should be cold, into boardgame-dice pieces and drop them in the bowl. Pinch and rub the butter through the flour until the little lumps of butter are blended in to make a fine crumb feel. Add the water, stirring round the inside of the bowl with a table knife until the dough comes together. Lift it out and knead it on a flat floured surface for 2 minutes until it becomes smooth. Wrap it in clingfilm and leave in the fridge to rest for half an hour at least.

Comes the time to make the empanadas, beat the egg with a little cold water. Working on a floured surface, roll the pastry out to about the thickness of a 20 pence piece, and then cut into five circles the size of a 7-inch single. (If you don't know what one of these is, ask your parents.) Place 2 good tablespoons of the filling in the centre of each circle. Dipping your finger in the egg/water mix, wipe it around half the circumference of your pastry circles. Pull the opposite side over on to the rim of the surface you have just wetted. Roll the edges in twice and pinch from end to end. Repeat this procedure until all the filling is used.

Get a large saucepan and fill with about 5cm vegetable oil, or turn your fryer on to 180°C/350°F. When the oil has come to heat – it must not be smoking, as danger in your kitchen will be impending – test the temperature by plopping in a little coin-sized piece of pinched-out pastry: it should whiz around, fizzling madly. Do not put the empanadas in until the oil is ready, otherwise they will sink and become uneatably greasy.

Pick the empanadas up carefully, as you will find they are quite fragile. Pop them into the hot oil, two at a time, and cook them on both sides until you achieve a dark biscuit brown. Remove them to waiting kitchen paper, using a slotted spoon. Please eat while they are hot. A good splash of hot chilli sauce suits them well, as does a very cold bottle of lager.

CURRIED MUSSELS WITH LOVAGE OR CELERY LEAVES AND LAGER

Lovage is a very distinctive herb that sadly has disappeared from our tables. It is easy to grow for anyone with an allotment or garden who appreciates a pastis-like aniseed-curry twang. Cultivated lovage looks very different from the wilder strains, which are a lot darker, the leaf more pointed. Celery is a more flimsy alternative compared with the unmistakable punch of lovage, but it still works. Lovage goes very well with white meats and most fish.

The lager you use should be very light, as a stronger one, coupled with the lovage, would make the sauce too bitter.

Serves 2

2kg mussels
6 small shallots or 2 banana shallots
2 celery sticks
1 garlic clove, peeled

a fat knob of butter
large-flaked sea salt and black pepper
1 level teaspoon mild curry powder
1 x 33cl bottle light lager
a small handful of lovage or celery leaves
100ml double cream (optional)

A sound thumping would be guaranteed if approaching any grizzled old fisherman and trying to pull his beard off, an indignity that sadly must befall the mussel when preparing it for the pot. Take the little wet tuft, or beard, sticking out of the side and pull it forward until it comes away. It can be obstinate as the mussel tries to delay your lunchtime. Next, scrape off the barnacles if necessary with the side of a cheap spoon. Rinse the mussels one last time. Discard any that remain open if tapped.

Peel, halve and finely slice the shallots, de-string and finely chop the celery sticks and finely chop the garlic. Pile them up together.

Get the butter foaming in a deep pot before adding the vegetables. Give a good grind of black pepper to the vegetable mix. Cook it all until soft on a medium heat and only then add the curry powder, ensuring you don't burn it. Throw in the mussels and pour over half a bottle of lager (drink the rest). Stir and put the lid on the mussels. Cook them for 4 minutes. Ideally you want all the mussels to have just opened but for the flesh to be very soft and not totally come away from the shell. At this point transfer them to the chosen bowl where they will finish cooking. Discard any that do not open.

Check if the sauce needs a little salt; it probably doesn't. Turn up the heat and rapidly simmer the sauce for 2 minutes more. This is a good time to add the cream, if using. Cook for a further minute. Pick a small handful of the lovage or celery leaves and chop it finely. Pour the sauce over the mussels and scatter the lovage or celery leaves over the top. Devour your steaming mountain of sweet plump mussels with slurps of soup and mouthfuls of crusty buttery bread, tossing the shells over your shoulder with abandon.

OYSTERS

I once visited an oyster farm in California, where shucked shells from harvested meat were used to lay a track to the highway. Lorries passing had powdered these shells, and a dust had floated up and settled over a kilometre in every direction. The landscape was nuclear grey and, until I realized what was going on, I approached the farm slowly like the couple driving towards their doom in a horror flick. I've tried clusters of tiny African oysters, delicate *fines de claires* and whoppers in Mexico, but the English and Irish natives are my favourites. It is their minerally twang, firm texture and meaty taste that are so good.

For those keen to try shucking, natives are easier, as they are more uniform in shape than rock oysters. When choosing a knife, a guard is good. Pick one that ends with a proper fine point; the other shapes are rubbish. Opening oysters needs calm. Take a heavy tea towel as protection. Fold it in half and lay an oyster on it, flat-side up, before folding the cloth over the top, exposing its hinge to your right hand. Push the knife hard into the dark crease of the hinge, holding the oyster down firmly with the left hand, hopefully protected by the cloth. Be deft and bold or the oyster will tighten up. Wiggle the blade as you push. Twist and there should be a popping sound as the hinge snaps. Imagining the tip of the blade against the roof of the shell, scrape the knife down the inside, severing the muscle that holds the two sides together. Remove the top. Release the oyster from the underside muscle and eat.

SMOKED OYSTERS

Here is a down-to-earth treat that delivers almost instant gratification. Smoked oysters are now widely available in most supermarkets.

Serves 1-2

bread, for toasting
butter

1 x 50g tin smoked oysters
lemon juice
freshly ground black pepper
cayenne pepper

Quite simply, toast the bread and spread on a generous amount of butter (don't be shy), applying oysters from tin to toast, taking with them a little of the oil as you go. Dress with lemon juice and black pepper and a pinch of cayenne. Cut the toast into quarters.

Serving portions are determined by how many tins of oysters you decide to take to bits of toast. I'm a heavy loader. Val's household ratio, one tin to one toast.

OYSTERS PO BOY

This is a very delicious but deeply unhealthy sandwich – but who cares. This is real cops-on-stakeout eating-in-car food. If you are worried, neutralize the effect with a dinner of grated carrots, or no dinner at all. Known as the 'peacemaker', this really will shut you up once you have finished it.

Serves 1

1 good soft bread roll (not crusty)

FILLING
6 rock oysters
3 tablespoons cornmeal
$^1/_2$ teaspoon cayenne pepper
large-flaked sea salt

1 medium egg, beaten with 2 tablespoons milk
100ml vegetable oil
2 tablespoons celeriac rémoulade (see page 190)
1 tomato, sliced thinly
2-3 thin slices of sweet pickled cucumber (gherkin)
tomato ketchup
hot chilli sauce (optional)
a few rings of raw red onion (optional)

Preheat the grill to full.

Shuck the oysters (see opposite) and leave to one side in their juice. On a plate, mix together the cornmeal, cayenne pepper and 1 teaspoon salt.

Heat the vegetable oil in a small frying pan. Get it nice and hot, but not smoking. Test the temperature by adding a small pinch of bread, which should frizzle immediately. If not hot enough, the oysters will soak up the oil, becoming soggy, greasy and unpleasant. Before frying the oysters, toast the halved roll lightly under the preheated grill, on the crust sides.

You are now ready to fry the oysters. Taking each one, dip it in the egg and milk, then roll it thoroughly in the cornmeal mixture. Pat off any excess. Fry the oysters until dark golden on both sides, about 2 minutes on each side. When done, transfer them to a good pile of kitchen paper to drain.

Ready to load. Dollop the rémoulade on the roll and spread it around. Pop the little oysters on top of this, gently lay over some thin slices of tomato and of sweet pickled cucumber and squeeze on a blob of ketchup and the hot chilli sauce, if desired. You can add lettuce; I don't like it in my burger, and I don't like it in my Po Boy – again, it symbolizes a limp gesture at health. Add the onion, if you like it raw. Then put the lid on and get involved.

FRIED OYSTERS WITH ATTITUDE SAUCE

Many think the cooking of an oyster to be a vulgar interference with its oceanic essence. I disagree. Cooked oysters are superb. When a moment of relaxed pleasure is impending, prepare these, ensuring that on consumption you have everything around you that you need, because when teamed with telly and cold bottled beer, a plate of golden fried oysters can often induce a deep, satisfied lethargy. These are excellent made with native oysters but, as they command the price they do, you can always use rock oysters instead.

Serves 1 (should serve 2)

6 large Atlantic rock oysters
2 tablespoons plain flour
large-flaked sea salt and black pepper
a splash of milk
1 medium egg, beaten
a handful of porridge oats
1 digestive biscuit
3 cream crackers or water biscuits

vegetable oil, for shallow-frying

ATTITUDE SAUCE
2 tablespoons tomato ketchup
a pinch of celery salt
$1/3$ teaspoon English mustard powder
2 drops of Worcestershire sauce
a squeeze of lemon juice
a dash of sherry, if possible
hot chilli sauce (optional)

Shuck the oysters (*see* page 118), and lay them on kitchen paper to drain of juice. This is important, as if they are too wet they will pick up too much flour. On a small plate mix the flour, salt and pepper. Next to that, put in a bowl the milk mixed with the beaten egg. Have one last little plate with a mixture of the porridge oats, finely crunched-up digestive biscuits and cream crackers and cornmeal. Roll each oyster in the flour, to evenly and lightly coat. Pat off any excess flour. Next, dip in the egg and milk mixture, ensuring total covering. Lastly, roll in the mixed oats and crumbs, and place on a plate (the waiting room). Repeat until all the little oysters are clothed.

Heat the oil in a small frying pan. If you use a pan that is too big, you will have to use far too much oil in order to achieve the 2.5cm depth of oil for the shallow-frying. When the oil is ready (test by dropping a pinch of porridge oats into the pan to see if they immediately frizzle), add the oysters, frying on each side for about $1^1/2$ minutes or until deep golden. When they are done, put them on a plate covered with folded kitchen towel.

While the oysters are frying, mix all the sauce ingredients together in a small teacup with a teaspoon. Perch the sauce next to the oysters, and make sure you have turned off the oil. Eat the oysters in a comfy chair.

NOTE: *If the oysters are shucked for you by the fishmonger, eat them on the day of purchase. However, when bought fresh in the shell and stored in the fridge, they have a good week's usage time. It's worth pointing out that if, on opening an oyster, you are at all in doubt as to its smell or look, discard it. It's never worth being poisoned through winging it.*

CRAB

BAKED CRAB CREAMS

This was my mother's invention, served at least 10 years ago, but it was so good it will never be forgotten. I can only hope that as she cannot remember how it was done, as I think my version is no flimsy imitation; it is pretty close to the original.

The onions found in the Alpine macaroni recipe on page 134 are an excellent topping for this crab dish. Prepare the onions before you start any of the crab processes.

Serves 6

250g brown crabmeat
2 medium eggs and 3 medium egg yolks
150ml single cream
large-flaked sea salt and black pepper
1 teaspoon Dijon mustard

150ml milk
a pinch of freshly grated nutmeg
butter, for greasing

TO SERVE
crisp onions (optional, *see* page 134)
toast and butter

Preheat the oven to 190°C/375°F/Gas 5.

Put everything except for the nutmeg, butter and black pepper in a blender and whiz for 10 seconds. Push the mixture through a fine sieve into a measuring jug, then grate in the nutmeg and grind in some black pepper. Stir.

Butter the inside of six 8cm ramekins before pouring in the mixture. Fill them right to the top. Put the ramekins in a roasting tin filled with 1cm kettle-hot water and pop in the preheated oven for 20 minutes.

Check to see that the creams are ready. Jiggle the tray and it will be apparent if they are not. You want a slight wobble, but not ripples. You can always remove one and dip in a spoon, as any damage will be covered by the onions (and you can serve this one to yourself if you wish). The closer to *only just set* it is, the better.

If they are done, remove each ramekin from the oven to a small plate. Sprinkle with the crispy onions (if you have included them). Serve immediately with a teaspoon and buttered white or brown toastlets to plunge into this quivering delight.

SPIDER CRAB FRY WITH PARSLEY, GARLIC AND LEMON

When fishing in autumn from Chesil Beach, my excitement as the rod tip judders often turns into disappointment as yet again I have tangled up an opportunistic spider crab. I am terrible at beach fishing, but have an uncanny knack of hooking spiders. Waiting for a bite, I will sometimes drift into a trance, engaged with the idea of the crab's eye view as it slowly creeps over the sandy floor towards my bait. They have strange thorny looks, but foolish is the man who dismisses them as bad eating. They make very good eating. The body contains little, but the legs are very tasty. You will need about three crabs for two people, and concentrated perseverance, as eating them is fiddly.

Serves 2

3 spider crabs
large-flaked sea salt and black pepper
about 60ml good olive oil

$^1/_2$ bulb of garlic, cloves separated
a large handful of parsley leaves or fennel
     tops, chopped
juice of 1 lemon
½ teaspoon dried chilli flakes

Heat a large pan of water, big enough to fit the crabs, and bring to the boil with a good amount of salt. Before plunging the crabs into their hot bath, I think it only fair to dispatch them first. Flipping them upside down, pull up the flap that protects their middle underside, and push a skewer into the small indent underneath. This will kill them immediately. It is also helpful, as their long spindly legs when alive and splayed out can prove very difficult to push into the pot. Put the crabs into the hot water and boil them for 5 minutes. Remove, allowing them to cool, and throw away the water.

Snap off the legs and claws and put to one side. Before throwing the bodies away, take off the top shell by prising the crabs open with a knife, discarding the main body, and pour in a little olive oil with a grind of black pepper and a pinch of salt. Rattle around with a teaspoon, scraping out the tasty mouthfuls you'll find within. Break the legs at the joints. Drape a tea towel over them and bash them with a rolling pin or hammer, but not so fiercely that you break each one to smithereens; you just want to crack each leg segment.

In a large pan, heat the remaining olive oil, throw in the garlic, which you have peeled and coarsely chopped, and fry it until it just begins to show the faintest traces of golden colour. Chuck in the chilli and crab legs and stir everything vigorously for a couple of minutes. Add the chopped parsley or fennel tops and squeeze in the lemon juice, cooking for a last couple of minutes as you stir everything around continuously.

Turn the whole lot into a bowl and descend on it like a gull. There is no place here for anything other than a crab pick and fingers, which you will spend a lot of time licking. This is fun, tasty but sparse, and you'd be well advised to have another course in the oven to follow.

SQUID

SQUID WITH CAPERS AND HARISSA

I am fascinated by these alien creatures, moving like ghosts in the black water of night, occasionally obliged to rocket away from stuffed and lazy sharks. Choose medium-sized squid, the body similar in size to an ice-cream cone, not big ones, as they can be a bit leathery.

Serves 2

2 medium-sized squid
good olive oil
large-flaked sea salt
1 lemon, cut into wedges

SALSA
2 lemon
1 handful of parsley leaves, finely chopped
1 large garlic clove, peeled and minced
1 teaspoon harissa paste
2 tablespoons baby capers, drained
black pepper
2 good tablespoons olive oil

Have the squid prepared for you. Keep the tentacles and the fins, and have the body opened out fully, having been sliced open down its natural groove.

Lay the squid body flat on the board, outside down (the outside is slightly more firm.) Holding the knife at an angle, slash the squid from one thick end corner diagonally to the pointed end; don't cut through it. The lines should be 1cm apart. Crosshatch in the other direction, again at a diagonal.

Scratch the zest off the lemon and mix it with the parsley and garlic in a bowl. Chop both ends off the zested lemon, putting it flat-side down on the board. Cut away all the remaining skin and exposed pith, leaving the fruit. Cut away the fruit segments from the skin that lies on each side, poke out any pips and add these segments to the salsa. Squeeze in the juice. Add the harissa and stir in the capers, pepper and oil.

Put a large frying pan on a fierce heat and get it very hot. Lightly rub some oil into the squid before generously salting the slashed side. Do the same to the tentacles and the fins. Place the squid in the pan, crosshatched-side down, ensuring none of the pieces are overlapping. After about a minute, the ends of the large squid pieces will begin to lift; if they do not, slightly help them by bending them over with your fingers. As the meat lifts from the pan it will roll itself into a binocular shape; fiddle with it to turn it into a tube. Flip over the tentacles to ensure they get a thorough cooking with the little fins. When done, there should be an orangey-brown to the outside, and a delicious smell drifting from the pan. The process will take about 3 minutes.

Take the squid tubes to the middle of each plate, drape over the tentacles and fins, and add the salsa, a little olive oil and a lemon wedge.

COCKLES

COCKLES WITH BACON AND CREAM

This is my favourite breakfast, leaving me incapable of sleeping in on waking up, knowing what awaits downstairs. The best bread to accompany this is toasted soda bread (*see* page **236**) or, if you really need to stoke the furnace, a fried and well-drained slice of white. This recipe is for freshly cooked and picked cockles, *not* the ones you find in jars of vinegar. You will occasionally find pre-picked cockles a little gritty. This can't be helped. Reserve any extra juice, straining it into a bowl. Flash the cockles briefly under cold water in a colander to wash away any sand. Do not soak, as they will become tasteless.

Serves 2

3 rashers of smoked streaky bacon
1 small onion, peeled
a knob of butter

150ml double cream
150g picked fresh cockle meat
large-flaked sea salt and black pepper
freshly grated nutmeg
2 slices of toast or fried bread, to serve

Cut the bacon into little strips and dice the onion finely. Gently fry the two in the butter for about **10** minutes. When the onion is meltingly soft and a little caramel-coloured, add the cream, cockles, a pinch of salt if necessary (you probably won't need it), a good grind of black pepper and the tiniest grate of nutmeg. Stir and, when the cream lightly simmers, race to the buttered toast or fried bread. Eat immediately, although you will hardly need any coaxing.

A BAD START TO THE DAY

Val Warner

CHEESE & EGGS

CHEESE

ALPINE MACARONI

On ordering this for the first time in a log shack as the snow wandered down outside, I felt peeved that my portion arrived in a pitifully tiny copper pot, hardly enough, it seemed, to satisfy the needs of my appetite. On completion, however, I smilingly announced that I had eaten one of the most outstanding and certainly richest pasta dishes of my life. I ordered another. If you make more you will eat more, so caution my friend, for after the gluttony will come your piggy remorse and total inability to move.

Serves 4

250g aged Gruyère cheese (normal will suffice)
25g butter
1 good tablespoon plain flour
200ml Riesling white wine
1 generous teaspoon German mustard
150ml single cream
large-flaked sea salt
150g rashers of smoked streaky bacon
300g dried macaroni

2 good cloves of garlic

CRISP ONIONS
2 medium onions
200ml vegetable oil (or enough to cover the bottom of your pan with 1cm oil)

APPLE SAUCE
3 Cox, Russet or Braeburn apples
125ml water
1 teaspoon caster sugar
white wine vinegar

Grate all the cheese and leave to one side. Take a large non-stick saucepan (for washing-up purposes) and melt the butter, not allowing it to burn. Add the flour to the pan and, using a whisk, thoroughly blend the two. (Using a whisk side-steps sifting the flour and ensures a lump-free sauce.) After the flour has foamed for about 20 seconds (do not let it brown), start adding the wine bit by bit. At first it will clag up, but don't be alarmed; keep on dribbling it in and whisking, and soon a velvety emulsion will start to evolve. Finish adding the wine. Introduce the cheese to the sauce and whisk it in until melted, followed by the mustard and cream. Season with salt and put to one side.

For the apple sauce, peel the apples, remove the cores and chop the flesh into small pieces. Put the apples in a pan with the water, sugar and a splash of white wine vinegar. Simmer, partially covered with a lid, until the apples have completely collapsed. Blend or mash to a purée and leave to one side.

While the apples are cooking, attend to the onions. Peel them and cut them in half, top to bottom. Lie them on their flat side and cut the thinnest slivers you can across the onion. Thinness is essential. If your stomach knots with impatience, take a deep breath and re-apply yourself. Thin, thin, thin.

In a frying pan, heat the oil until it's hot enough to immediately frizzle one of your onion slices. Add half the onion slices, making sure they are not piled up but spread evenly over the pan. Regulate the heat if they start colouring too fast, and continually move them around the pan to ensure even cooking. Watch them intently. The desired result is dark golden onions. There will be blackened onions here and there, but this is to be expected. When they have achieved this colouring, after about 4-5 minutes, immediately lift them from the oil with a slotted spoon to a waiting area of kitchen paper. Resting here, they will drain and become totally crisp. If they are not, you have either cooked all the onions together, as instructed not to, or you have panicked and taken them out too early. Repeat all this with the second batch of onions. As this is the only refined element to this dish, take time. It's fiddly, but the end result is worth it. Leave to one side. Do not pour used oil down the sink.

Cut the bacon into 1cm strips and add them to the cleaned frying pan. Add a tiny bit of oil just to get the bacon going. Fry until it is nearly crisp. Transfer to more kitchen paper.

Nearly there. Put water on to boil for the macaroni. Put the cheese sauce on a low gas and slowly bring it to heat, not letting it catch. Do the same with the apple sauce. Put the macaroni into boiling water with a big pinch of salt and cook until it is done. *Al dente* is nothing to do with this dish. The macaroni wants to be cooked through, but not so that it's mushy.

Remove the cheese sauce from the heat. Drain the macaroni thoroughly, then add it to the sauce. Add the bacon and garlic (leave it out if it is nothing short of exceptional) and mix well. Turn the whole lot into an appropriate serving pot. Scatter the onions all over the top, but do not mix them in. Put the lid on the pot and take it to the table. Eat immediately with a large spoonful of hot apple sauce dolloped in the middle of each serving and then retire to the sofa and fall asleep with a newspaper over your head.

CAULIFLOWER CHEESE

Another book with cauliflower cheese in it – boring. Well, I hope not. This one has big shards of smashed crispy Cheddar jutting out of the browned saucy cauliflower. Squint at it and miniaturize yourself, an explorer mountaineering across this dramatic cheese landscape.

Serves 4

1 large cauliflower
large-flaked sea salt and black pepper

CHEESE SAUCE
30g butter
2 tablespoons plain flour

1 heaped teaspoon English mustard powder
300ml milk
170g strong mature Cheddar cheese
Worcestershire sauce
a hint of freshly grated nutmeg

CHEESE SHEET
80g strong mature Cheddar cheese

If any of the cauliflower leaves appear a little grizzled, snap them off and discard them. Snap off the remaining leafy stalks, but keep them with the cauliflower. Split the cauliflower with a knife, dividing it up into about eight large pieces.

Put a pan of salted water on to boil. Once the cauliflower and stalks are in the water, let it come back to the boil and cook it for 5 minutes. Drain the cauliflower and allow it to cool. Make sure it is really well drained, as excess water will ruin the sauce.

Take the pan you have just used. Don't bother to wash it, but make sure there are no cauliflower bits inside. On a medium heat, melt the butter before stirring in the flour and mustard powder with a whisk. Do not let this brown, but cook it gently for about 40 seconds. Whisk in the milk, pouring it in bit by bit. Let the white sauce gently bubble while you grate in the cheese. Add a splash of Worcestershire sauce, the nutmeg, then assault it with a big grind of pepper. Put the sauce to one side.

Preheat the grill to full.

Now for the cheese sheet. Don't rush this stage, as it takes a little longer then you think. Grate the Cheddar. Put a non-stick frying pan on a medium heat. Sprinkle in the cheese, covering the surface of the pan with a thin layer. It should not be piled up, but evenly distributed, with no obvious large gaps. (Made too thickly it will not crisp properly and be a bit chewy in the middle. *Wrong.*) The cheese will start to melt. Cook it for about 4 minutes. If the fat from the cheese starts to smoke, turn the heat down. Work a spatula under one edge of the sheet to see if it lifts a little. If it does, get the edge with your fingers, lift the sheet and turn it over. If it stretches rather than lifts,

leave it a little longer. It will momentarily hurt your fingers. Nothing you can't handle, though. Be deft not hesitant, or the sheet will buckle and fold. Cook on the other side for a couple of minutes. This sheet of cheese should be taken out now where it will cool and immediately become crisp. You'll want to nibble it, but don't; you'll eat it all and there'll be none left.

Place the drained cauliflower in a suitable oven dish. Whisk the sauce one last time to blend in any skin that has formed, and pour it over the cauliflower. Slide it under the grill, not too close to the orange element. Allow the top to brown and the sauce to bubble, about 10 minutes.

Divide on to warm plates before breaking, not smashing, the cheese sheet. Place the pieces artfully around each serving.

WELSH RAREBIT

This dish has attitude and a strong flavour that twangs the roof of the mouth. It knocks out cheese on toast, barely before they have touched gloves. Cheese on toast is all well and good, but a bit of Cheddar fainted on some weedy bread quickly becomes pathetic, the sad crusts regular visitors to the bin, whereas Welsh rarebit – proper!

Serves 2

25g butter
1 heaped tablespoon plain flour
100ml stout
a good splash of Worcestershire sauce

1 teaspoon English mustard
150g mature Cheddar cheese
black pepper and/or cayenne pepper
2 good large slices of brown farmhouse
    bread

Melt the butter in a pan on a low heat. (Non-stick will help with the washing up.) When it is foaming, add the flour and blend it into the butter with a whisk. Whisks help to eradicate lumps, so I would commend them over spoons. Cook for about 30 seconds, but do not brown the flour, or you will have to start again. Add the stout bit by bit, whisking all the time until you have a nice smooth, brown, creamy paste. Cook for 2 minutes. Stir in some Worcestershire sauce, and not that two-drop nonsense: get some in there.

Stir in the mustard before grating in the cheese. When it has been melted and stirred in over a low heat, finally add some black pepper. You may also add a dash of cayenne pepper. I don't, but you choose. This mix shouldn't really need any salt, as the cheese will contain plenty. The sauce should be quite thick. Of course you can use it immediately, but if you have the time to cool it in the fridge, when you apply it to the toast cold, heating up slowly, the outside browns under the grill, forming a delicious skin that does not allow the middle to run out.

Preheat the grill to full on.

Toast the slices of bread, but not too heavily. Dad always said burnt toast would keep my hair curly, and I had no choice. Don't burn the toast! I would not bother buttering it, as there are quite enough fats in the sauce already. Take as much mix to the toast as plaster to a bare wall. Don't be shy! The bread should be well covered.

Pop your loaded toasts beneath the grill until your rarebit is browned and bubbling. A champion among snacks, I think you will agree?

PEAR AND ROQUEFORT SALAD

I'm sorry if you have seen this starter many times before, but I love it. So this is for those who may not have eaten this wonderful combination, or a memory jog for those who have simply forgotten about it. To make a really good one, the ingredients must be top notch. The Roquefort should have a pokey strength, saltiness and that faint gritty texture with a good amount of blue. The pears should be very sweet, juicy and with a smell hinting of nail polish remover. Make sure the salads are excellent, with young, firm chicory and bright green, pert lamb's lettuce. For those who find cooking a little difficult, this is an easy but impressive salad to serve.

Serves 6

50g Puy lentils, rinsed
14 walnut halves
6 fresh dates
2 small chicory heads
2-3 large handfuls mâche (lamb's lettuce)

2 large ripe pears
a generous splash of good-quality
    sherry vinegar
good olive oil
large-flaked sea salt and black pepper
125g Roquefort cheese

Gently boil the lentils in a small pan for about 20 minutes, until tender but not over-soft. Drain in a sieve and set aside. While the lentils are boiling, put the walnut halves in another small pan and cook over a medium heat, turning regularly until lightly toasted. Tip on to a plate and leave to cool.

Stone and chop each date coarsely into about six pieces or so. Trim the chicory and separate the leaves before tearing them into two or three pieces. Rinse the leaves with the lamb's lettuce. Dry in a spinner or with kitchen paper and toss together in a large serving bowl. Peel, halve and core the pears and slice them lengthways into slivers the width of a £1 coin, adding them to the bowl.

Splash the good sherry vinegar about the leaves and pears with a generous trickle of olive oil, a grind of pepper and a small sprinkling of salt. Be careful with the seasoning, as the Roquefort is salty by nature. Turn these ingredients over gently until they are mixed well and lightly coated with the vinegar and oil. Do this carefully so as not to damage the mâche, which bruises easily. If a little flat, lift the salad in the bowl, as gently as a grabbing claw in an amusement arcade, so the leaves appear airy, bouncy and alive.

Scatter over with the lentils, walnuts, dates and finally pieces of cheese, crumbled or pulled from the block and not chopped into boring squares. Make sure some of the cheese nestles within the salad and does not just sit in a heavy pile on top. It is important to assemble the salad only just before serving, otherwise, although dressed, the chicory and pear will discolour and the leaves collapse, the dish resembling something you might eat at a wedding.

EGGS

SCRAMBLED EGGS DONE PROPERLY

Of course, everything is a question of taste, but scrambled eggs with milk breaks my morale before the day has even started and reminds me of bad B&Bs with bacon oozing white water and a virtually raw grilled tomato. Small relief in not eating this so-called scrambled egg can be found in sculpting it into barely amusing shapes. Here's a better version.

Serves 2 (in hope that I have company at the weekends)

2 thumb-sized knobs butter
5 good large free-range eggs, beaten
large-flaked sea salt and black pepper

On a low heat, melt the butter in a non-stick pan (as it makes cleaning easier). When the butter has melted a little but not completely, add the eggs, some salt and a good fine grind of black pepper. Keeping the pan on a low heat, stir the egg constantly and thoroughly, getting into the corners and bottom of the pan. While doing this, meditate on how much you love someone or how sweetly the robin sings. After what seems a fair while, your wrist will be slightly sore and the eggs will start to coagulate. Pay attention, for this moment is critical.

When all the egg is cooked, with no glassy jelly bits, but the texture still loose (this is why it should be cooked slowly), it is done. As it hits the plate or the toast, a little slow spreading should be witnessed as the eggs move into position. Eat immediately.

A small plate of these bright yellow scrambled eggs covered in shavings of fresh black summer truffle (which grow well into the autumn) is amazing. Only beaten by the white Alba truffle.

SPROTTLED EGG

What a funny name, what a tasty breakfast. If you are not a fan of anchovies, simply remove them from the recipe and send them to me.

Serves 1

butter
enough double cream to cover the egg

1 large egg
2 good salted anchovies, washed and
    roughly chopped
large-flaked sea salt and black pepper

Preheat the oven to 180°C/350°F/Gas 4.

Smear the inside of a suitably sized ramekin with a little butter. Pour double cream halfway up the inside, then break in the raw egg. Splash a little more cream on top so that the yolk is just covered with cream to prevent it from drying and overcooking. Drop two tiny knobs of butter around the egg with the pieces of anchovy and then add a little salt and a grind of pepper.

Put the ramekin in a small oven tray with 1cm kettle-boiled water in the bottom. Bake in the preheated oven for 15-20 minutes, until the white has set but the yolk remains runny.

Eat with buttered toast.

EGGY PANETTONE

I never seem able to cut one of these fluffy sweet breads, but normally rip it limb from limb in the passenger seat of the car while driving home from the shops. However, at more restrained moments I achieve this gentler treatment.

Serves 1

1 slice panettone
1 large egg

2 tablespoons milk
a fat knob of butter
plum jam or maple syrup

Cut yourself a slice of panettone. Combine and then vigorously beat together the egg and milk in a bowl, creating a good froth.

In a pan, heat the butter. When it is hot and foaming (but it must not be smoking), dip the slice of panettone in the eggy mix on both sides and flop it in the pan, frying it gently and flipping it when golden. (Make sure the panettone doesn't spend too long in the egg mixture; you don't want it to be like a wet sponge.) Fry the other side.

When done, take the bread to a plate and smear it with a ridiculous amount of plum jam or maple syrup.

ROOT, STEM & LEAF

MUSHROOMS

MUSHROOMS ON TOAST

I'm crazy for mushrooms on toast, often cooking them with my overcoat still on, scarf dangling in the pan, in my eagerness and excitement to get them on to the toast and into my mouth. The following ideas are not so much a recipe, as how hard can frying mushrooms be? However, there are a couple of things I would like to point out.

With the lawyer's wig (or shaggy ink cap), if you have the good fortune to gather enough, then use them alone. They literally have to be raced back to the kitchen as, once picked, they visibly collapse like a fatally wounded general, fading before his adoring troops. Unlike other mushrooms, I would not fry them hard, as the dark and exquisite juices they leak are very tasty and, cooked too much, you will be left with little juice or flesh. So the toast in this instance becomes more of a mopper-upper.

With the firmer varieties, however, I like to achieve some browning in order to really accentuate the woody, mossy, mealy or meaty tastes achieved by reducing the juices. Blewits, girolles, yellow legs, ceps and trompettes respond well to a harsh heat. Varieties such as the pied de mouton (hedgehog mushroom or fungus) actually require a hard fry, as eaten in their own juice they can taste a little insipid. Large parasols and field mushrooms, looking so splendid in their size, I would not slice at all but cook them whole, draping a couple over and obscuring the toast. These also would do well with a browning in the frying pan or under the grill, as it is hard to dry them out, while staying juicy within. The trompette, a curious little fairy instrument, is very good but needs combining with other varieties. Some mushrooms are better with the juices reduced, while others should be celebrated for their inky leakings.

The puffball is a curiosity and one easily spotted from miles away, the size of a child's football, a distant beacon shining from the grass. It is an acquired taste, but I like it. Puffballs, although keeping their shape, do not last as long as you might think. They need to be eaten fairly swiftly on picking. Simply slice like a loaf of bread and fry in butter. Acting similarly to a sponge, it is tempting to keep on adding butter as it gets absorbed in the pan, but be careful, for when ready you will suddenly find you have a very 'greazy' slice. So I would suggest just one good knob of butter, added in two parts when you flip it over. Plonk it straight on to the toast. Grind over slightly more pepper than you normally would, and add a squeeze of lemon.

Quite often, it is hard to pick a puffball before someone's child races past you and boots it into a million pieces.

I would on the whole suggest not adding wines or vermouth to mushrooms. With some varieties offering such subtle tastes, muffling them seems to ruin the point rather. That said, strong mushrooms, namely the boletus family, go very happily with a splash of this or that when playing a role in a more luxuriant dish (*see* the chicken with penny bun sauce on page 54).

A little garlic is very nice, but with wet mushrooms it is better added raw afterwards, finely chopped with parsley and perhaps a little lemon zest. I have to say I prefer my mushrooms with curly parsley. Cream or a dollop of crème fraîche – yippee! But it does depend on the mood.

Now for the toast. The perfect vehicle for mushrooms. It should have a good crunch, as it will fade once wet and under-toasted soggy bread is not that fun.

So much writing for something so simple – excuse me!

BAKED MUSHROOM AND CELERIAC TORTE

Like Fred and Ginger, the celeriac and the mushroom dance very well together. A class act for an evening's entertainment… or lunch. Oh! And this is very delicious eaten entirely on its own.

Serves 2-4

1 small celeriac
400g girolles, yellow legs or oyster
    mushrooms

2 garlic cloves, peeled
2 sprigs of fresh thyme
50g butter
large-flaked sea salt and black pepper
100ml single cream

Preheat the oven to 220°C/425°F/Gas 7.

Don't prepare the celeriac until you want to use it, as, left sliced while you are distracted by *Strictly Come Dancing* or other weighty matters, it will discolour fast to punish you for loving it one minute and ignoring it the next.

Go over the girolles or other mushrooms carefully, taking care to cut away, pick out or brush off any mosses, soil or bugs reluctant to leave. Chop the garlic into tiny pieces, mix it with the thyme leaves, stripped from their stalks, and leave on the board until needed.

In a frying pan, heat a small knob of the butter and fry the mushrooms hard. At first they will be swimming in their own juices. It is most important that this is banished from the pan, so keep on frying them until they become coloured and the liquid is gone, gone, gone! Throw in the chopped garlic, salt to taste and the thyme, and stir through the mushrooms, keeping them on the heat for another minute or so. Put to one side.

Generously grease a separate non-stick, ovenproof frying pan, about 15cm in width, with a little of the remaining butter, and season with a little salt and pepper.

Cut the skin away from the celeriac. You will have to cut a little deeper than with other roots, as the outside of this vegetable tends to be woody and fibrous. Split the celeriac in two. When you have cut it in half, you may find a little hollow in the middle. Don't panic, this is perfectly natural.

On a mandoline or slicer, or with a strong and sharp knife, slice each half of your celeriac crossways into thin slivers.

Using half of them, one by one arrange them in an overlapping star shape around the bottom of the pan. Remember to cover the hole that will be left in the middle. Obstinate celeriac slices might not bend perfectly round the sides of the pan at first but, after the mushrooms have been added and the plate on top, which will follow shortly, they will do what they are told. Flop in your mushrooms and arrange them in their arena. Pour over the cream.

Arrange the rest of the celeriac slices over the top and dot with the remaining butter. (If you find that you have cut too much celeriac, the rest can be shredded and used in celeriac rémoulade, *see* page 190, although it will need to be put in water with lemon juice to stop it discolouring.)

When you are ready to cook, turn the hob to full and put the pan on the heat. Wait until you hear some cooking sounds and then leave the pan there for about 4 minutes. This ensures that what will be the top of the turned-out dish will be well browned. Put a hardy plate that fits the inside edge of the pan over the top of your torte before placing the whole shebang in the preheated oven and cooking it for 20 minutes. When cooked, a skewer should push easily through the celeriac.

Remove the plate from the top and, with a spatula, run the tip round the inside of the pan to help the contents to release easily when the dish is turned out. Now turn it out. If it doesn't go according to plan, don't worry. It might not impress your loved ones, but the important thing is that it will taste just as delicious.

WILD MUSHROOM LASAGNE

This makes a comfortable block of flats for mushrooms to cohabit with sheep's curd, and spinach if it's in town. The ingredients are few, as I tend to enjoy mushrooms when tampered with as little as possible. Although there are some good dried lasagnes, making fresh pasta is a meditative and soothing pastime, so go and get a pasta mangle. Remember that you don't have to ignore this recipe because you don't have any wild mushrooms. You can buy selections or simply replace them with cultivated ones. The use of olive oil in this recipe is hard to measure and all I would say is that you should be generous when frying the mushrooms and spinach, and sparse when assembling the lasagne. You will have to use your judgement.

Serves 4

PASTA
300g Italian '00' plain flour
200g semolina flour
large-flaked sea salt
4 medium eggs
2-4 medium egg yolks
(or dried pasta; follow the pack instructions)

FILLING
1kg wild mushrooms (*see* below)

3 garlic cloves
3 good sprigs of fresh thyme
olive oil
1kg spinach
freshly grated nutmeg
50g Parmesan cheese, freshly grated
300-350g sheep's curd or soft fresh
     goat's cheese
freshly grated black pepper
50ml single cream

The pasta must be made first, as it needs to relax in the fridge before use. In a food processor, place the flours and a good pinch of salt and turn on the power. Start by adding the whole eggs, and then the yolks, one by one. As soon as the crumbs start to cluster and ball, you have added enough egg yolks. Whop the lot on to a work surface gathering all the stray parts together until you get a crudely assembled mound. Knead the pasta for approximately 2 minutes using the ball of your thumbs and base of your hands to work it. Manipulate it into a block and, when done, wrap it in clingfilm and place it in the fridge. Leave it for an hour or so.

Clean your mushrooms carefully, as there is no room for critters or dirt. Tear large girolles or over-sized oyster mushrooms, as it seems more appropriate than cutting them. Leave small ones as they are. Ceps, blewits or field mushrooms will need slicing. But try and cut them so that they keep their shape; it's nice to see things as close to their natural form as possible. Put them to one side.

Peel the garlic and strip the thyme sprigs. Chop the garlic and thyme leaves together until the garlic is very fine. Heat a good slug of olive oil in a frying pan and wait until it is very hot before throwing in the mushrooms. Fry

them hard with a teaspoon of salt, getting rid of the juices that seep out, until they are nicely and richly browned. This is important, for if you build the lasagne with watery contents, you will be left with a soggy disaster and a bad opinion of vegetarian food. So take the time. For the final minute, throw in the garlic and thyme, thoroughly stirring it in. Transfer the mushrooms to a bowl and put to one side.

Get a big pan of water on to boil. It must be large to ensure the pieces of pasta are not crammed together in the water like farmed trout.

Wipe the mushroom pan clean, adding another good slurp of olive oil. Get this hot before throwing in the washed and drained spinach. It will crackle and spit, collapsing very quickly. Stir it vigorously. When entirely limp, which will happen in little more than a minute, grate over a little nutmeg and pinch over some salt, stirring in well. Transfer the spinach to a colander and, with the back of a spoon, press out all its water. Press it hard chanting 'Water out! Water out! Water out!'

To roll out your pasta, fix the pasta machine firmly to the edge of the table. Scatter some semolina flour over the surface on which the pasta will lie. Cutting a playing-card-packet-size slab of the dough, wind it through the largest setting. As it comes through the other side of the press, gently place your hand under it and help it out as you wind, otherwise it will pile up like laundry and problems will arise. If you notice the pasta ripping, you could be pulling it too much or it could be too wet. Don't worry, guide it all through, letting it rest on the flour. This will stick to the pasta and help it dry a little, rather like sticky pastry on a floured work surface.

Fold the pasta end to end and, winding the folded end first, put it through again. Doing it this way always ensures that any air bubbles are forced towards the open air. Click the setting down by two and repeat the process, going through twice each time, using the semolina flour where necessary. Finally, wind it through the thinnest setting.

Laying the entire length out flat, cut it into sheets about 13cm long, making sure they rest side by side and not on top of each other. Cut and roll some more dough, and repeat the process until all the pasta is used and you have a lot of lasagne sheets.

One by one, drop the sheets into the boiling water and cook them for approximately 2-3 minutes. They need to be cooked while retaining the slightest bite. Drain them in a colander, then cool them under running cold water. Drain again. Mix through with a little olive oil, which will help prevent them sticking.

Preheat the oven to 200°C/400°F/Gas 6.

Choose a deep oven dish rather than a wide one, as this will enable you to make a deep, three-floored lasagne rather than some wrong-looking pancake affair. Wipe some olive oil around the inside of the dish before scattering it with a sparse layer of grated Parmesan (reserving some for later). Lay a few sheets of the pasta over the bottom, all slightly overlapping. Scatter some mushrooms about and then some of the goat's cheese, broken into lumps. Lay on some spinach. Thinly pour over a little olive oil and grind over some black pepper. Repeat until all the components are used. The last layer should be pasta. Press down on the top with a spatula to compress your layers slightly. Pour the cream over the top with a final slug of olive oil. Dust over with the remaining Parmesan.

Place the dish in the preheated oven and cook the lasagne for around 30-40 minutes. Devour.

AUTUMN PASTEL

This pie, or pastel, has accompanied me on many excursions with rod and gun. It uses the same stuffing as you will find in the cabbage on page 169. Occasionally, I will serve this hot from the oven alongside a rib of beef. Pushed around in gravy, it is a highly effective mopper-upper and stylish alternative to Yorkshire pudding or potatoes.

Serves 4-6

375g rough puff pastry (*see* page 249)
plain flour, for dusting

1 recipe mushroom filling (*see* page 169)
1 large egg yolk
a dash of milk

Have the pastry made and rested beforehand. Make the filling. Preheat the oven to 200°C/400°F/Gas 6.

Flour your largest kitchen work surface and roll out the pastry, keeping it floured and flipping over when necessary. Don't roll it out so thin that it tears while you are filling or moving it. It needs to be rolled into a huge rectangle, approximately 60 x 40cm, narrow width facing you. Make sure there is flour under it so that it can be easily moved and not torn when ready for the oven. Just below your imaginary centre line, turn out the filling and form it into a neat, low-sided brick shape, leaving plenty of room around it.

When this is done, beat the egg with the milk and, taking a pastry brush, paint a 5cm band around the two sides and edges of the filling nearest you. Fold the top over and press lightly all the way round over the border you have glued and sealed with the egg, as no room for escape is permissible. Work from one side to the other so that any unfilled empty pockets are ushered out. Cut off the excess pastry, leaving a 2.5cm border around the pastel, and then crimp this with the end of a fork.

Slide the pastel on to an oven tray lined with baking paper, introduce it to the preheated oven and cook for approximately 25 minutes. When it is a beautiful golden brown around the edges and a slightly darker shade on top, remove from the oven and paint the roof evenly with the rest of the egg mixture, then return it to oven for a further 3 minutes. It is now ready.

Serve the pastel either hot or allow it to cool on a wire rack and take on a later adventure.

RAW MUSHROOM SALAD

Raw mushrooms can be delicious and, in the months of heavy eating, a welcome relief. This recipe works best with young, firm, pale mushrooms, as if made with inky varieties the contents of the bowl can look none too appetizing. So for this recipe I would suggest your using young cep mushrooms, girolles, young, tight and firm field mushrooms that have only just appeared in the grass.

Serves 2

350g wild mushrooms
1 excellent fat garlic clove, peeled

juice of ½ lemon
excellent olive oil
large-flaked sea salt and black pepper
a little chopped parsley and mint

Clean the mushrooms very carefully, keeping back any damaged ones for stocks or stews, as this dish requires the finest specimens. Taking a sharp knife, slice any capped mushrooms into thin slivers from side to side. Tear girolles from the head end into small pieces.

Put all the mushrooms in the bottom of a non-metallic mixing bowl. Split the garlic in half lengthways and slice both pieces incredibly finely, as if you were going about it with a magnifying glass and a razor blade. Turn the garlic through the mushrooms. Squeeze over the lemon juice and add 3-4 large tablespoons good olive oil with 1 teaspoon sea salt and an enthusiastic grind of black pepper. Mix everything thoroughly again before leaving the whole lot to stand for a minimum of half an hour. The acid in the lemon juice will in effect cook the mushrooms.

Just before eating, chop a small fistful of parsley with a small fistful of mint, and mix it through the mushrooms. Arrange a handful of mushrooms in a dainty pile on a plate and finish with a little extra good olive oil. So delicate, so pleasing, no cooking. This is also great as a bruschetta.

LENTILS

I enjoy my post-cinema channa dhal with naan, but have often found other lentil dishes to be an alarming mush and the invention of those who would also eat broccoli and pasta bake. Once on a silent retreat we were forced to eat lentils almost every day and, trying to enter the spirit of things and attempt a little yoga as well (which incidentally seems to bring on mild panic), I found the uncomfortable positions – coupled with lunch – to be a one-hour exercise in trying not to let rip. However, the exquisite tiny Puy lentil is one variety that I love dearly, consume in healthy amounts and is seemingly less windy.

Beware other wee lentils in poncey ribboned packets from obscure parts of Europe. Although delicious, they seem to command ridiculous prices that make you hand them straight back to the shopkeeper with your nostrils flaring. These are best eaten in situ. Puy lentils should be cooked gently and retain a slight bite, not to be confused with undercooking. Wash the lentils before using to clean away that European dust and check for any stones.

PUY LENTILS WITH CHANTERELLES AND BACON

Both the following recipes, one hot and one cold, go very well with all meats, especially game, and also sit happily beside a large piece of fish.

Serves 4

175g Puy lentils
2 bay leaves
3 shallots
2 carrots
2 garlic cloves
2 small celery sticks
10 rashers of smoked streaky bacon

a good slug of olive oil
2 large handfuls of chanterelles (girolles)
    or tube chanterelles (yellow legs)
large-flaked sea salt and black pepper
a good dash of red wine vinegar
extra virgin olive oil
a small fistful of fresh parsley or tarragon
    leaves, chopped

Put the lentils with the bay leaves into a pan and cover with cold water. Bring them to a rapid simmer and then discard the black water and refill with more cold water just above the line of the lentils. Simmer gently for half an hour, adding a little more water if they appear to need it. You will know when they are ready by spooning a few into your mouth. They should hold their own shape and have a little bite to them, but not be resistant in the centre.

In the meantime, peel the shallots, carrots and garlic and de-string the celery. Chop all of these into a teeny-weeny fine dice. Take the rind off the bacon, if it exists, and chop the bacon into thin slivers.

Heat the olive oil in a frying pan and get the bacon off to a head start. When it just begins to colour, add the vegetables and cook until they are totally soft and the shallot just begins to take on a golden appearance. Add the chanterelles now. The objective here is to no more than wilt these fragile things and impart their delicate mossy taste without hammering them.

When the lentils are done, put them in a sieve and drain them. Add them back to the pan and stir in the bacon and mushroom mixture. Check the seasoning, adding a little salt and some black pepper. With your thumb covering most of the bottle exit, splash a little red wine vinegar (two to three shakes) over the lentils and cook on a low heat for a further 5 minutes. Add a little extra virgin olive oil and the chopped parsley or tarragon, depending on what is available.

Serve this earthy dish with the chosen mainstay, although it is also delicious eaten on its own

LENTIL VINAIGRETTE WITH CHICORY

If you are a fan of grown-up bitter tastes, then here's a delicious dish that celebrates chicory as well as lentils.

Serves 4

4 medium banana shallots
175g Puy lentils
2 bay leaves
large-flaked sea salt and black pepper
a large fistful of fresh parsley
2 small heads chicory

GARLIC VINAIGRETTE
1 big fat hard garlic clove
1 level tablespoon Dijon mustard
2 teaspoons caster sugar
1 capful red wine vinegar
juice of $1/2$ small lemon
5 tablespoons olive oil

Peel and finely chop the shallots, splitting them in half and cutting thinly from end to end. Put them in a pan with the lentils and bay leaves and cover with water. As in the previous recipe, throw away the first batch of water on boiling and refill the pan, covering the lentils with fresh cold water. Simmer them gently for about half an hour, but taste them to make sure they are done; a little resistance in the skin, but cooked and giving inside, is the aim. Drain them thoroughly in a colander.

Meanwhile, for the vinaigrette, peel and then chop the garlic very finely with a good pinch of salt to help it break down. Put it into a small mixing bowl and flick in the mustard before adding the sugar, vinegar and lemon juice. Add the olive oil and beat the mixture with a fork until it becomes creamy.

When the lentils have cooled, put them in an attractive bowl and season with salt. Lentils will take a fair amount of salt to reach full flavour but it is always better to taste as you add, bit by bit. Finely chop your washed and dried parsley and mix it into the lentils well. Post-mix, tidy up any mucky edges on the bowl.

After discarding any unsightly outer leaves, slice the chicory as thinly as you can from tip to toe. Don't cut the chicory until just before it heads off to the table, as it will discolour over time. Scatter the chicory over the lentils, allowing them to be glimpsed here and there. Pour the garlic vinaigrette in an artful way across the top of the salad. Mix at the table. Very good with guinea fowl roasted with rosemary and sherry.

PUMPKIN FAMILY

Should I ever escape the urban corridors of town, I intend to fully embrace pumpkin fancying. It really is a magic seed with its lush leafed and dewy tentacles crawling out over the ground to capture any hint of moisture and send it back to the fat baby.

That big bum of a thing lying heavy in the soil huge and orange, what a great return for the little pip pushed with a finger into the ground. So often the subtle taste of pumpkin is obliterated with spices and this is a shame. Stick your head inside one and inhale deeply. Melony, wet, refreshing – it is delicate and so should be treated in accordance.

When my time comes, rather than leave a few garish brass handles lying about underground, I think I should like to be lowered down in my hollowed-out record-breaking pumpkin with the rosettes fastened to my lapel and pumpkin soup served back at the house.

DAD'S PUMPKIN SOUP

The delight this soup used to cause my brother and me seemed immeasurable. Dad would tie on his stripy pinny, which always struck me as a faintly ridiculous look for a man of six feet five, and then close the kitchen door. Muffled crash, bang, tinkles would be heard through the house as the special soup was created by the master. Finally, it was time to eat it and in he would carry the whole pumpkin to the excited table. Holding the stalk, the top would come off and the billow of steam would shoot up. God it was good, the theatre and the eating. More, more, more!

Serves 8-10

1 x 4kg pumpkin
2 medium onions, peeled
125g butter
1 cinnamon stick

freshly grated nutmeg
1-2 level teaspoons large-flaked sea salt, to taste
black pepper, to taste
1.7 litres chicken stock (*see* page 246)
3 tablespoons sherry

Carefully cut a lid off the pumpkin and keep it. Remove the seeds and fibres from the middle (keep the seeds for roasting and salting). Carefully hollow out all the flesh with a knife and a spoon. It is imperative that you do not cut right up to the inside of the skin or pierce it, as it will no longer be usable as a tureen; scrape and cut into the pumpkin up to no more than 2cm to the inside. When all of the flesh has been removed, roughly chop it and put it to one side.

Chop up the onions nice and finely. Melt the butter in a large pan and throw in the onions, cooking them slowly until they are soft, about 15 minutes. Add the pumpkin flesh and all the remaining ingredients except for the stock and sherry. Put the heat to medium and the lid on the pot, occasionally stirring the contents to avoid it catching, until the pumpkin is cooked through, about 40 minutes.

Add the stock and then either blitz the mixture with a blending stick or in a food processor. Bring the soup to a low simmer and cook for a further half an hour.

45 minutes before eating, preheat the oven to 170°C/325°F/Gas 3.

Pour the soup into the pumpkin shell and stir in the sherry. Put on the lid and bring the soup up to heat in the preheated oven: this will take about 45 minutes. Lift the whole pumpkin on to a suitable tray and carry it to the table, with a ladle. You don't have to bolt the soup before midnight; it will not be drawn away by a team of harnessed white mice.

STUFFED MARROW

The marrow has been rather forgotten, poor thing. People just don't seem to know what to do with it. It has a wonderful taste, a combination of pumpkin and courgette. I remember the stuffed ones my mother used to carve up at the table, all piping hot and steaming. Because of their water content, although firm, they do need a lot of gubbins in the middle so that the stuffing-to-marrow ratio is correctly balanced. So you will need at least 1kg of stuffing to a 2kg marrow.

I have gone slightly Eastern bloc on this recipe, as I think the raisins, cinnamon and smoked paprika work well. I have used beef shin, which I've braised and shredded, getting away from the usual inclusion of mince (I prefer mince in a burger). It is simple and pleasing, and goes well with a cold lager. Although the overall cooking time is lengthy, each stage is very simple. When cooking the beef, the marrow I refer to is that in the bone of the beef shin (of course you can leave it out if you wish). This is a game of two marrows.

Serves 4-6

1 x 2kg marrow

STUFFING
1.5kg good beef shin on the bone, chopped into 3-4 pieces (by the butcher)
olive oil
1 large onion, peeled
2 good garlic cloves, peeled

$^1/_3$ cinnamon stick
1 small teaspoon cumin seeds
2 heaped teaspoons *pimentón de la Vera* (hot smoked paprika)
finely grated rind and juice of $^1/_2$ lemon
1 conservative handful of raisins
1 x 400g tin chopped tomatoes
$^1/_2$ tomato tin water
a heavy, heavy grind of black pepper
100g stale bread
1 teaspoon celery salt
2 heaped teaspoons large-flaked sea salt

Select beef shin pieces with a good lot of bone marrow, as this is tasty and keeps the meat moist when cooking. Get a large lidded flameproof casserole, put it on a low heat and pour a generous slug of olive oil into the bottom. Put in the pieces of shin. Finely dice the onion and garlic, then add to the pot. It is not the aim to brown the meat at all but to let everything slowly come to heat and cook gently. Chuck in the remaining ingredients, except for the bread and both salts. Put the lid on the casserole and turn the largest gas flame or hob to as low as it can go, just so that the stew is bubbling away slowly in the pot. Cook this for 3 hours.

Smash up all the bread to crumb size in a food processor or by any other method necessary. (If it is not totally stale, not to worry, but you really don't want fresh bread; if it is new and soft, rip it up and dry it out a little in the oven.) Put the crumbs to one side.

When the shin has braised, allow it to cool completely. When cooled, pick up the meat, which should easily come away from the bone. Pinch each piece between thumb and forefinger to break it up and string it out a bit. Throw away any unsavoury bits, but not before you have extracted every last bit of meat. Do this over the sauce so that the meat falls back in. Make sure any marrow hiding in the bones has also been poked out into the meat and gravy. Try not to eat it all. Season the filling with the salts. Don't be alarmed by the amount of salt, as marrow dishes need it. Add the breadcrumbs to the pot, where it will firm up the sloppiness, giving the stuffing a nice texture.

Preheat the oven to 200°C/400°F/Gas 6.

Split the marrow evenly down the middle from end to end (you would be wise to choose as straight a marrow as possible, as it will be easier to deal with than one that is skew-whiff). With a spoon, scrape out the seeds and pith from down the middle of each marrow half.

Double over and lay a sheet of foil across an oven tray, with long enough sides overlapping the tray that they might be gathered round the assembled marrow and folded on top. Oil this sheet lightly where the marrow's underside will sit. Place the marrow on the awaiting foil. Fill the marrow with as much of the meat stuffing as you can. Don't worry, the foil will keep all present and correct. (If the filling is fridge-cold, bring it to room temperature first; otherwise you would have to overcook the marrow.) Gather

the foil round the middle of the marrow and fold over on the top to secure all. Yes, I realize the ends of the marrow are sticking out. Cook the marrow in the preheated oven for 35-45 minutes; it is cooked when a skewer slides in with the tiniest resistance, but not like a knife through warm butter.

It can be tricky to release the marrow from the foil once it has been cooked. Put the whole thing on a serving dish with the foil and open it at the table. Cut in slices, and there you have it. Eat with cold bottled beer.

WARM MARROW WITH CARAWAY AND MUSTARD

This is a tasty little salad in its own right, but it will also go very well with a roast chicken or duck confit.

Serves 2-3

1 x 500g marrow
good olive oil
2 teaspoons caraway seeds

large-flaked sea salt and black pepper
2 good teaspoons German mustard
1 capful red wine vinegar or juice of $^1/_2$ small lemon

Peel and deseed the marrow and then chop the flesh into chunks the same size as half a small matchbox.

Put a frying pan on a medium heat and add a good slug of olive oil. The oil must not smoke. Add the marrow chunks and a generous splash of water. Stir around the pan, and after 4 minutes, when the water has evaporated, add the caraway seeds and a generous pinch of salt. Cook for a further 3 minutes. Add the mustard (French mustard would be a second best), and toss the marrow in the pan until it is well coated.

With your thumb over the top of the bottle, splash about some red wine vinegar or squeeze in the lemon juice. Add some black pepper and adjust your salt seasoning.

Eat while it is warm.

CABBAGES AND OTHER LEAVES

Maybe even more than beetroots, cabbages get bad press, the word 'school' ringing through the mind like the lunchtime bell. To me the real villains, after the cooks that is, are steaming pots of furiously rolling water into which the chopped cabbages, silently pleading and moaning, are lowered and crammed to cook until unarguably lifeless. This may seem like an old argument, but there is still a lot of bad cabbage out there. Don't get me wrong, boiled cabbage can be delicious. But cooked lid on and forgotten long before the meat is ready? I just can't help myself and have to step in. My jaw is gritted and the host gets nervous. It's a bad business.

It doesn't take much to think of hot, tasty, glorious mouthfuls of buttered cabbage, luscious coleslaws idling over fat burgers, shredded green leaves dropped into goosey broths and sharp sauerkrauts to cut flavoursome fats. A little more brassica consciousness, please, as it can be one of the finest vegetables known to man.

CABBAGE STUFFED WITH MUSHROOMS, LEEKS, STILTON AND WALNUTS

Although you have to use your imagination, what I love about this is the idea of deconstructing something in order to rebuild it back into its likeness. At this time of year, I fill the cabbage with autumn treasures, all time-honoured old friends. Brought to the table, it's a crowd-pleaser, especially for vegetarians (although I rarely have a crowd of vegetarians in my house). For this recipe you will need a 1.5-litre pudding basin and a large lidded pot to accommodate it. You will also need two discs of cardboard cut to fit the inside top of the bowl, wrapped together with foil.

Serves 4-6

1 large Savoy cabbage
butter

MUSHROOM FILLING
500g collected field mushrooms, blewits and/or girolles (or chestnut mushrooms)

30g butter
large-flaked sea salt and black pepper
$1/2$ teaspoon freshly grated nutmeg
2 medium leeks
100g shelled walnuts
200g mild Stilton cheese
3 Medjool dates

Choose a handsome large cabbage. Take the dark green outer leaves off carefully, throwing away as few damaged leaves as possible. Be kind; a little leaf distress is no matter. Keeping as close to the stalk as you can, cut only the thickest part of it from each leaf, as they need to be kept whole. You will want to go two layers into the cabbage and you'll need eight or nine leaves.

Bring water to the boil in the pot in which you will be steaming the stuffed cabbage. Dip the leaves in for 30 seconds to make them pliable (not to cook them). Remove the leaves from the water with a slotted spoon, avoiding ripping them, and rinse under cold water. Shake the leaves before laying them on a tray lined with kitchen paper. Layer more paper between the leaves.

Start the mushroom filling. Wipe the mushrooms clean and finely slice them, stalks and all. (Do not use Portobello, as they turn the whole filling an unappetizing colour.) Melt the butter over a medium heat in a frying pan and, when foaming, throw in the mushrooms. Add a good pinch of salt, the nutmeg and a bombardment of black pepper. When you think that's enough, add two grinds more. Fry the mushrooms until all the water has evaporated and they begin to catch and take on a rusty brown colour. Take time to do this, as swimming in a pool of water they are not ready for the stuffing.

While the mushrooms are cooking, remove two outer layers of the leeks' skin and trim off any ragged tops. Split the leeks lengthways and wash under the cold tap. Make sure they are clean, as mud, sand and grit will ruin a good thing. Dry on kitchen paper, split lengthways and chop finely, about 5mm thick. Add the leeks to the mushrooms only when they have achieved the colour and dryness explained above. Mix together and keep on the heat until the leeks are cooked and their moisture has been banished skywards. When they start to catch, they are done. Excess water will spoil the consistency of the filling. Preheat the oven to 200°C/400°F/Gas 6.

Chop the walnuts into small pieces (but not in a blender, or they will turn to dust). Put them on a tray and pop into the oven. *Don't forget them*. Having incinerated a fortune in nuts, I advise you to set a timer! When they are golden and smell toasted, they are done; 5 minutes, let's say. Rub the walnuts lightly in your hands to shed as much of the skin as possible.

Cut the cheese from the rind and crumble it into the cooking leeks and mushrooms. When the cheese is distributed and fully melted, turn off the heat and add the nuts. Stone and chop the dates, add them to the mix and stir in with the nuts. Leave to one side in the pan. Make sure the dates are well mixed in, as they can tend to clump together.

Prepare the cabbage. Lightly butter your 1.5-litre basin. This does nothing for the cooking of the cabbage, but helps the clingfilm to stick when you are lining the bowl. Leaving plenty of overhang, drape four lengths of clingfilm in a criss-cross fashion so that the whole bowl is covered, the layers of clingfilm overlapping to create a strong skin. Taking one leaf of cabbage, place the bowl on top of it and cut around its base to fashion a circle to fit inside the bottom of the bowl. Put to one side. Take the remaining leaves, remembering that the outside of the leaves should face the inside of the bowl. Not willy-nilly, but trying to make a similar pattern to that of a naturally grown cabbage, distribute the leaves around the inside of the basin, overlapping. Insert your cabbage circle in the bottom. (There should still be a couple of leaves left to cover the open top of the bowl.)

Pack the stuffing into the cabbage casing, really patting it down and filling it up, but leaving 3cm exposed around the top edges. With your remaining leaves, cover the top. Picking up the clingfilm edges and, working round slowly, pull in the clingfilm, which in turn will fold the sides of the cabbage in on its lid. Twist all the clingfilm into a tight knot; it must be sealed.

Bring the pot of water back to a simmer; it should be a third full of water. Place your foiled cardboard disc on the cabbage and put weights on top (cleaned stones from the garden would do). Put the basin in the pot, add the lid and steam for 20-30 minutes. Adjust the heat so the water is still simmering even with the lid on. To turn out, open up the clingfilm and pull it to the outside of the basin. Place an upside-down plate over the top and, wearing oven-gloves, invert the basin on to the plate. Lift off the clingfilm and basin. A little water will run on to the plate; mop it up with kitchen paper. Take the cabbage to the table, where everyone will look the picture of happy surprise you might find on a board-game box. This dish looks pretty when the green cabbage is surrounded by slices of pink ham.

RED CABBAGE DONE PROPERLY

I live in hope that any red cabbage be treated well, but on the whole my heart sinks. Yet again it arrives at the table like a waterlogged inkblot of dark lilac misery. Here is the secret. *Do not boil.* Take a breath and exhale your old method. Send your '70s copy of *50 Country Lunch Favourites* to the charity shop. Here we go.

Serves 6

1 medium red cabbage
40g butter
large-flaked sea salt and black pepper

3 bay leaves
4 cloves
100ml white wine vinegar
25g unbleached white sugar

Remove any offending outer leaves from the cabbage and discard them. From stalk to top, split the cabbage in half down the centre. Cut out the main part of the white core inside. Cutting across the cabbage, shred it from top to bottom as thinly as you can. Rinse the cabbage under cold water in a colander and let it drain. The object of this is to only take the amount of water left on the cabbage to the pan.

Get a big heavy-bottomed pan that can easily accommodate all the cabbage. Put it on a large ring at full heat and get the butter in. When melted throw in all the cabbage. You should hear a frying sound and this is good. Add 2 teaspoons salt, a heavy grind of pepper, the bay leaves and the cloves. Cook it like this for about 10 minutes, stirring often and adding a flick of water here and there.

Now add the vinegar. Step away briefly as the initial steam shoots up, or you will be staggering backwards from the stove scraping your eyes and screaming AYE! Vinegar steam is unpleasant. You will notice that once the vinegar is stirred in, it snatches back the vivid purple of the cabbage. Keep on cooking and stirring until all the vinegar has evaporated. You should not see any loose vinegar in the bottom of the pan.

Only when it has completely evaporated should you sprinkle in the sugar. You must watch the cabbage now like a hawk would for mice. In the absence of water, the sugar will melt and start to caramelize. Keep on stirring it and moving it around so that each sliver of cabbage rests only fleetingly on the bottom of the pan. If you ignore it, the sugar will catch and things will start to burn. Keep the contents on the move.

After 5 minutes of constant attention, the cabbage should be done. Taste it. It should have a pleasant sweet and sour taste, a moistness with a bit of bite and be something that you would not try to hide beneath your knife and fork.

PATA NEGRA AND SAVOY CABBAGE SALAD

This is a delicious salad, and one that I learnt under the tuition of Alastair Little, a great and generous teacher who showed me the delicious pastures beyond the bowels of *haute cuisine*. It is a pretty salad and so easy to make, almost instant gratification, but it's imperative that the cabbage be fresh and crisp and the ham good. I like the pata negra ham from Spain because you can really taste the acorns that have been gobbled up by those black-trottered pigs snuffling beneath the oaks.

Serves 4

$^1/_2$ medium Savoy cabbage
8 slices of Spanish cured ham (*jamón iberico* or *pata negra*)

good extra virgin olive oil
sherry vinegar
large-flaked sea salt and black pepper

Remove the outside gnarled leaves from the cabbage. Keep the inner darker ones, as they contain that good irony taste. Cut out and discard the stalky bit and wash the leaves. Dry them thoroughly. Lay the leaves on top of one another, roll them up and very finely slice the roll from end to end. Shred the remaining paler piece of the cabbage half, having cut out the stem part. Put all the cabbage in a mixing bowl.

Unwrap the *jamón* and slice this into 1cm ribbons. Prevent the ham pieces cling to each other by cutting each slice individually and adding it to the cabbage as you go.

In a thin stream, pour a generous amount of good olive oil about the salad. Splash the sherry vinegar about a bit too. You certainly want the twang of the vinegar, but not so that you screw up your face on the first bite. Taste a little as you dress the salad and doctor it accordingly. Add the seasoning. The coarsely ground black pepper should be present in each bite, but the salt must be administered carefully, as the *jamón* will lend its own saltiness to the dish.

I think this is a salad that is best assembled on each plate as opposed to arriving in a large bowl. I don't know why, it just is.

COLESLAW

This is more of a chopped cabbage than a coleslaw. Rather than making an extravagant mayonnaise with olive oil and Dijon mustard, here we'll take a shortcut, shop-bought mayo being more appropriate for this recipe. This is an almost essential accompaniment for the pork on page 26; make it while leaving the pork to its business.

Serves 6

1 small white cabbage
1 level tablespoon caraway seeds
4 heaped tablespoons shop-bought
   mayonnaise

juice of $^1/_2$ lemon
1 heaped teaspoon German mustard
1 good teaspoon caster sugar
a good pinch of large-flaked sea salt

Discard any unwanted outer leaves from the white cabbage. Split it down the middle from top to bottom, cutting out the core. Lay it on a board, flat-side down, and slice it across in 1cm ribbons. It is not necessary for you to cut it too finely.

In a dry frying pan, carefully toast the caraway seeds. In the bowl in which you intend to serve the coleslaw, combine everything apart from the cabbage before mixing the cabbage through.

Let it rest for half an hour before you plan to eat it.

CREAMED SPINACH

Creamed spinach, if it's there, cold or hot, I just can't leave alone. I have cut my tongue licking the blender blades. It's definitely a contender for the 'if you could have one last meal' game. By the time my green-fingered skirmishes are over, I've never made enough. Always make extra.

Two rules: it must not be watery, and it must be green – green, not the overcooked colour of Fidel Castro's romper suit. I like the older, bigger leaves for this, which have a stronger mineral taste. And if your garlic is soft and has sprouted, leave it out of the recipe altogether.

Serves 4

1kg young spinach
a fat knob of butter
1 heaped tablespoon full-fat crème fraîche

2 tablespoons olive oil
1 excellent garlic clove, peeled
   and crushed
freshly grated nutmeg
large-flaked sea salt and black pepper

Wash the spinach thoroughly and then drain it in a colander. Take a pan large enough to take all of the spinach and get it on a high heat. Melt a fat knob of butter. When the butter is hot, not smoking, chuck in all of the spinach, a couple of handfuls at a time. Spit, crackle, sizzle it will go. Stir away, turning the leaves until all pertness has totally collapsed, adding more as you go.

This process will only take a couple of minutes. Turn off the heat. Pressing the spinach against the side of the pan with a wooden spoon, tip away all the excess water. Stir the spinach and repeat the process, getting rid of more water. Really press that spinach as dry as you can, then put it in the blender. On top of the spinach flop in the crème fraîche, olive oil, raw garlic, nutmeg, salt and pepper. Be careful with the nutmeg: it lends such a good edge to spinach, but can ruin it if too much is used. Blitz everything up together until the purée is totally smooth. Adjust the seasoning to taste.

Heat it up just before you need it. If kept on a slow heat, it will lose its fabulous colour. Creamed spinach is a perfect accompaniment for a fat t-bone steak, pile of chops or hunk of white fish.

SWEET AND SOUR CHARD

Chard is for me like one of those people you really like but for some unknown reason forget to invite for dinner. I always seem to eat it in other people's houses and rarely my own. But it is delicious and not to be compared with spinach, being so distinctive in its gentle taste and soft but firm stalks.

Serves 2-3

50g golden raisins or sultanas
3 tablespoons extra virgin olive oil
2 medium white onions
3 fat garlic cloves

50ml white wine vinegar
1 teaspoon of caster sugar
25g pine nuts
a large handful of Swiss chard,
    roughly 8 large leaves, stalks removed
a pinch of *pimentón de la Vera*
    (hot smoked paprika)

Put the raisins or sultanas in a small bowl and cover with just-boiled water. Leave in the water until it is cold and they are needed.

Heat the oil in a medium frying pan over a low heat. Peel and halve the onions lengthways and then very finely slice them, before peeling and thinly slicing the garlic. Add these to the pan and cook very gently for about 15-20 minutes until they are meltingly soft but not at all coloured. Drain the raisins or sultanas and add them to the onions with the vinegar and sugar. Cook for a few minutes more, until the liquid has evaporated, then set aside.

Toast the pine nuts in a dry frying pan over a medium heat, jiggling the pan often to keep the nuts on the move, preventing them from burning in one place. When they have taken on a dark golden hue, allow them to cool on a plate.

Bring a large pan of water to the boil. Wash the chard leaves really well to remove any grit or indignant insects. Split each leaf through the centre and plunge into the boiling water. Cover and cook for 4-5 minutes until tender.

Drain the chard thoroughly in a colander, shaking it to remove any excess water. Really get it as dry as possible. Eaten at room temperature the chard is also delicious, so if need be, rinse it under cold running water first.

Arrange the chard on a serving plate and sprinkle over with some good salt. With your hands, arrange the onion mix over the top, making sure it is all placed well. Sprinkle the pine nuts about. Inspired by a trip to Barrafina, an excellent tapas establishment, I ate a Spanish version of this recipe called 'coca'. Made with spinach and resting upon crispy dough, it was dusted with a little hot smoked paprika. An excellent addition!

LEFTOVERS: *This recipe is excellent if leftovers are gently fried up with some coarsely broken tinned sardines, a little extra garlic and then tossed through some boiled spaghetti with a few extra pine nuts added on top.*

FRIED KALE WITH SESAME AND GARLIC

The hardiest and most vitamin-packed of all the late-year greens, kale is powerful stuff, and I'm surprised Popeye stuck with spinach. Full of minerals and with a good irony tang, it has real taste, but is better eaten younger as big leaves can be obstinate in the mouth. This is good with roast chicken and goose.

Serves 3

1 large hand-gathering of kale leaves
2 tablespoons sesame seeds

olive oil
3 garlic cloves, peeled and finely sliced
large-flaked sea salt and black pepper
a squeeze of lemon juice

Wash the kale well, expelling any small creatures, grit and other undesirables. Chop it into 1cm wide ribbons, discarding any stems that appear stringy. In a frying pan, toast the sesame seeds until golden, stirring often to prevent them from burning. Turn up the heat and add 2 tablespoons of olive oil to the pan before throwing in the kale, which will spit and crackle frantically. Stir it around, occasionally flicking in some water to keep the moisture content up. After about 2 minutes the kale will have collapsed. Now throw in the garlic. Keep everything moving around for another 3 minutes, until the garlic is just beginning to brown. Transfer to a plate and sprinkle with a little salt and pepper and a squeeze of lemon juice.

FENNEL

FENNEL PURÉE

Fennel is a magical vegetable, with many medicinal merits as well as delicious recipes to its name. With the tops cut down and the short stalks sticking up, the bulb almost resembles a heart and valves, heavy, firm and white, a clean heart, helping digestion, preventing gout and purifying the liver, help I certainly need or will. Eat more fennel!

I consume tons of it, raw in salads, combined with the seeds in cleansing teas or simply roasted. But when puréed, slowly spreading outwards beneath a weighty hunk of fish or lamb, I enjoy it most of all.

Serves 4

2 large fennel bulbs
a large knob of butter
2 tablespoons olive oil

2 garlic cloves, peeled and coarsely
    chopped
100ml dry white wine
100ml water
large-flaked sea salt

Trim the fennel bulbs and discard any damaged outer parts (unless it is in good nick, as the exterior can be de-strung). Reserve any nice green leaf tops. Roughly chop the fennel.

Melt the butter with the oil in a pan. Add the chopped fennel with the garlic. Cook briskly over a medium heat for at least 10 minutes, stirring every now and then until softened. The pieces will start to brown and this is fine.

Add the wine and water, cover with a lid and continue cooking for a further 10-15 minutes, until the fennel is very soft. Remove the pan from the heat and purée the whole lot using a stick blender or food processor until smooth. Season with a good pinch of salt. (A small splash of pastis can be a delightful addition.) Stir the chopped raw feathery leaves of the fennel through the purée.

This is especially good when accompanying the lamb with bitter herbs and honey on page 21.

ONION FAMILY

I revere the onion. It is definitely in my top three favourite vegetables alongside broad beans and beetroots. The backbone of so many cuisines, onions go quietly about their business, ungrudgingly playing second fiddle. Shop-bought, they can be poor, yellowing and gnarly, quietly sprouting on the shelf, but when chosen carefully and not taken for granted, they are generous and wholly essential to so many dishes that would be flat without them.

Tiny little pearl onions dotted throughout a coq au vin, refreshing salsas spiked with shallots, the snapping crunch of a pickled onion plucked from a ploughman's, the gentle flavour of white onions draped over fish; whether raw, fried, burnt, pickled or boiled, they are all great, beautifully packaged and, considerate to the last, will store well.

Try an onion baked with salt, pepper and butter. Roast it hard. Place it in the middle of your largest white plate, stare at it intently and consider it, but not so as to let it go cold. Enter the onion.

ONION TART

When I remember the taste of this tart, the first thing that pops into my head is not the eye-rolling delicious sweetness of the onions, but the image of a dusty track leading to tanned naked French girls lying unashamed on hot sunlit rocks rising from a cold mountain river. Château Double near Cannes was where we ate the tarts, however, it was a swim in the rock pools that had me smiling underwater, popping up like a 10-year-old seal to get another peek.

But the tarts, a second thought, *wow*, they were good too! It's why we went there. Eaten in the square beneath the shade of the plane trees, they could not be beaten. I have not been back there for 26 years, but am sufficiently happy that the following recipe is not a far cry from those tarts I speak of. Naked girls and onion tarts, how could a day be better spent?

This recipe really is about not rushing the onions. There is a lot of chopping to do, and they take some time to cook, but it beats most other onion tarts hands down.

Serves 8

14 medium-large onions
125g butter
1 cooked savoury pastry case
    (*see* pages 248/9)
100ml white wine vinegar

2 level tablespoons soft light brown sugar
1 teaspoon Dijon mustard
2 heaped teaspoons large-flaked sea salt

TO FINISH
50g Parmesan cheese, freshly grated
black pepper

Peel and dice the onions to superfine, or as small as you can. The finer you chop them, the better the texture of the tart. Take a large heavy bottomed lidded pan and in it melt the butter over a low heat before adding the onions and cooking on a low-medium heat. Get them cooking with the lid on. They should cook slowly, needing the occasional stir. You want them to be completely soft before you start adding any more of the ingredients. This will take about 2 hours.

While the onions cook, turn your attention to the cooked pastry case (*see* pages 248 and 249), which will cook at 200°C/400°F/Gas 6. Keep the oven on when you have finished it.

When the onions are totally and pathetically soft, turn up the heat and add the vinegar, sugar, mustard and salt. The vinegar will take some time to evaporate, but check the onions regularly: once the vinegar is gone they will begin to catch as the sugar starts to caramelize. Keep on stirring at regular intervals and adjust the heat so that the onions turn a rich brown but do not burn. A little colour from the bottom of the pan is OK, just stir it in. The vinegar/sugar stage will take approximately half an hour.

Fill the cooked pastry case with the onion mixture and smooth it out evenly with a spatula. Sprinkle with a faint dusting of grated Parmesan and go over with a good grind of pepper before cooking it in the preheated oven for 20 minutes.

Leave to rest to 10 minutes. Eat while warm, although it is also very good cold. And it might be worth doubling the recipe, as the tart is hard to leave alone once made I seem to keep on having just one more slice.

BILL'S ONION

Sitting in the heather, honking of stag and talking of food we did and didn't like, my deerstalker, keen to champion the Scot's kitchen, contributed the following. It's immensely pleasing to eat. (Though whenever I eat it, the recollection of Bill's deeply disturbing 'flip ma false teeth inside oot' trick can ruin the experience.) I have called it Bill's onion. I hope his wife or otherwise the inventor of the original version of this recipe is not offended.

Makes 4

4 small onions
1 portion of flaky pastry (*see* page 249)
2 medium eggs, beaten with a
    splash of milk

60g butter
2 level teaspoons soft brown sugar
large-flaked sea salt and lots of
    black pepper

Preheat the oven to 180°C/350°F/Gas 4.

Peel and top and tail each onion, cutting away a little more than one normally would. Then, with two deep cuts not quite going all the way through the onion, make a cross in the top of each.

Divide the pastry into four. Roll each piece out on a floured surface to the thickness of a one-pound coin. Cut each piece into two squares that are considerably wider all round than the onion (the bottom squares being approximately 12cm and the top approximately 16cm). Have the beaten eggs and milk in a bowl nearby with a wee brush.

Sit one of the onions on one of the pastry squares. Wedge about 15g of the butter into the slits in the onion. Sprinkle $1/2$ teaspoon sugar, some salt and a really big grind of black pepper over it. With the egg and water mix, paint all the way round the base edges of the pastry square.

Picking up another pastry square, place it over the top of the onion and push the edges gently on to those of the bottom pastry square. Taking a fork, crimp the edges all the way round.

Repeat this process with the other onions. Before putting them in the oven, paint the pastry with the egg wash to gloss them up.

Line an oven tray with some baking paper and lift the wrapped onions on to it. Cook them for approximately 45 minutes, until they are dark golden.

These complement a stew most highly, but they are good on their own as well. Do eat them hot, though.

LEEKS VINAIGRETTE

This is my favourite salad. It's calming to prepare and eat, a kind of cooking meditation. It is one of the few things I eat very slowly. It is so elegant and pretty in its colours, a feminine dish.

Leeks need so little doing to them before becoming delicious. I will never go **AWOL** (absent without leeks), as I always have some in the kitchen. Choose medium leeks for this recipe, not the club-sized things you would expect to see a Welshman banging against his shield as he taunts the enemy. Leeks have a habit of getting good mud deep between their leaves. Clean them well, as brown has no place in a dish that should be only white, yellow and green.

Serves 2

6 medium leeks
large-flaked sea salt
2 small eggs
a fistful of picked parsley leaves, finely
   chopped

VINAIGRETTE
1 heaped teaspoon Dijon mustard
a squeeze of lemon juice
2 capfuls tarragon or white wine vinegar
1 teaspoon caster sugar
50ml good extra virgin olive oil

Take off the outside layer of the leeks. Chop off all but 10cm of the dark green end (keep this portion for making leek and potato soup). Really wash them well. Trim the little beard from the end if there is any; do not completely chop off the soil end, as this helps to keep the leek together. If very long, chop each leek in half along the middle.

Get some salted water on to boil. Cook the leeks for long enough so that when the point of a knife is rested on them the weight of the knife naturally slides into the flesh. The leeks should offer no resistance to the blade; they must be soft to the cut and to the teeth. This should take about 7 minutes.

When ready, lift the leeks from the hot water into a colander sitting over a small pan. Do so carefully – if you have cut them in half, as the greener part of the leek cooks, each inner layer when handled might have the tendency to slip from the centre like a telescope. Don't throw the water away. Lay the leeks against the sides of the colander with the root ends uppermmost rather than flat across its bottom, as this will allow the water to drain out. Run a little cold water over them to cool them.

Using the leftover leek water, gently boil the eggs for 7 minutes until hard. When done, put them in a bowl of cold water to cool completely, as grating a warm egg is never particularly successful.

Turn your attention to the vinaigrette. Mix the mustard, lemon juice, vinegar, sugar and a pinch of salt in a bowl before slowly beating in the olive oil with a fork. It will emulsify into a creamy consistency.

It is time to assemble the dish. In the centre of a plate – I like a large white one – stack the leeks in a triangle like a log-pile. Peel the eggs, separating the white from the yolk. Grate the white on the medium setting of the grater before grating the yolk in the same way. Lovingly spoon the vinaigrette over all the leeks before sprinkling over the egg yolk, parsley and egg white, in three separate coloured bands. Destroy the pile instantly with a fork.

ROOT VEGETABLES

VAL'S POTATOES WITH DUCK FAT, GARLIC AND PARSLEY

This is my favourite potato dish of all time, but it *is* rich, and should you be rushed into hospital clutching your chest, the simple fact that you decided to cook it is my disclaimer for any cardiac distress caused.

Serves 4

1kg potatoes (Maris Piper or King Edward)
2 teaspoons large-flaked sea salt

80ml good dry white wine (eg Macon or white Burgundy)
150g duck or goose fat
2 handfuls of chopped fresh parsley
5 large, good and hard garlic cloves, peeled and finely chopped

Peel and cut the potatoes into small cubes the size of board-game dice. Put the potatoes into a pan of cold water with the salt. Bring to the boil and simmer rapidly until the cubes are well cooked, but still holding their shape. Drain thoroughly.

Transfer the potatoes to an appropriately sized non-stick frying pan so that they are not too thinly spread out, but are evenly about 2.5cm high. Splash the wine over them and put dollops of duck or goose fat around them. Place the pan on a medium heat and melt the fat; the melted fat should just be visible below the top of the potatoes. If the fat comes over the top pour a little off, and if it is not visible, add a little more. Fry the potatoes quite briskly for approximately 20 minutes (but not stirring at any point), by which time they will be done and the duck or goose fat should have been absorbed. Check for doneness by shaking the pan, with an ear close to the potatoes: you should hear a resonant scratching sound, signifying that the potatoes are crisp on one side. When you have accomplished this, slightly press the exposed side of the potatoes down, crushing them a little. They should be golden and crisply armoured on one side, soft on the other. Gently tip off any fat not absorbed by the potatoes.

Either invert on to a plate, using an upside-down plate on top of the pan and then flipping it over so that the crispy armour faces the eaters, or simply use a spatula to achieve the same end. If, on turning out the potatoes collapse a little, it's not really the end of the world.

Cover with the chopped parsley and garlic and serve immediately. These are fabulous served with beef on the bone and a salad that is wearing a sharp vinaigrette.

AUTUMN/WINTER SALAD

If you don't like anchovies, then kindly move along please. Call this salad
what you will to suit the month, but don't say 'autumn slash winter salad'.
That's just daft.

This is another pearler I learned in the kitchen of Alastair Little.
The dressing will always do what it is told, but cannot be heated up again
once cooled, as it splits with enthusiasm. Because this salad does require the
dressing to be warm, it must be made just before it is needed. The ribbons
of vegetables look very pretty: all Jackson Pollocked about with painterly
splashes of this exceptional dressing. The dish is a dainty one to prepare and
outstanding in taste.

Serves 4

3 medium carrots
4 Jerusalem artichokes
2 large celery sticks
juice of 1 large juicy lemon
2 medium trevise lettuces
a little dried hot red chilli
large-flaked sea salt and black pepper

good olive oil

DRESSING
400ml milk
4 garlic cloves, peeled
1 large sprig of fresh rosemary
8 anchovy fillets, drained
200ml olive oil

Pour the milk into a non-stick pan and drop in the garlic and rosemary. Put it
on the heat and bring it to a brisk simmer. Keep an eye out though, as, given
the chance, the milk will boil over like invaders pouring over a castle wall.
Make sure you regulate the heat accordingly. You want to reduce the milk by
approximately two-thirds, down to 120ml. Ignore the unsightly milk-skin,
old-spider-web look, as this will all become a beautiful creamy sauce; just
push any skin down into the milk with a wooden spoon. The reducing process
will take about 25-30 minutes.

Release the anchovies from their tin or jar and drop them into the
food processor or blender bowl. If the anchovies are tadpole-sized, throw in a
few more. Personally, I like the whole ones cured in chunky salt (wash and
de-bone them first).

Wash and peel the carrots and artichokes and destring the celery.
Retaining the peeler, shave all the vegetables lengthways in ribbons into a
large bowl of cold water clinking with ice-cubes. This will make them super-
crisp. Squeeze in half the lemon juice, to stop the artichoke discolouring.

Deconstruct the Trevise lettuces. Having thrown away any damaged
outer leaves, the Trevise, with its tight leaves, shouldn't need washing. Tear
each leaf into about four pieces and throw them into a large mixing bowl.
Do this one by one until the leaves become too small to carry on. Chuck the
last ones in whole. Repeat with the other lettuce.

In a salad spinner, or by other means, dry the shaved vegetables very well. Add them to the lettuce. Finely crumble over a little chilli (some flakes would do), add a pinch of salt and squeeze over the other lemon half. Pour over 2 tablespoons good olive oil. Mix everything gently and thoroughly before dividing it evenly between the plates.

Remove the milk pan from the heat and take the rosemary stem out. Pour the reduced milk, the rosemary leaves and softened garlic into the food processor or blender, all over the waiting anchovy fillets. Do not scrape the bottom of the milk pan, as any burnt 'catchings' will not blend properly and the sauce, that should be really smooth, will become bitty. Turn the power on high and in a thin, thin stream start pouring in the olive oil. After a while you will begin to see the sauce thicken. It is easier to tell how thick your mixture has become by stopping the blades and seeing it settle. When it has reached the consistency of a yoghurt drink or loose mayonnaise, it is done. Remove the blades and flick 2 good tablespoons about each plate of salad. Eat your 'autumn slash winter salad' immediately.

LEFTOVERS: *As the dressing chills it will thicken. It is delicious on hot bread and with strong dark meats such as roast beef and venison fillet, as well as next to a good crispy hunk of fish such as grey mullet.*

CELERIAC RÉMOULADE

There are two things I will say immediately about celeriac rémoulade: it should be properly pokey with mustard, and it does require you to make mayonnaise from scratch. Although you can cheat by adding the usual gang to some shop-bought mayonnaise, strangely I think I am letting the side down if I do it here. I do feel you can hurt ingredients' feelings once they know what they are going to be part of.

This is very good with cold chicken, and certainly a star player in the po boy sandwich (*see* page 119). It is also delicious when piled on toast with a mountain of white crabmeat, slices of smoked eel or a mound of carefully peeled, juicy prawns.

Serves 6

500g celeriac
200ml home-made mayonnaise (*see* page 112)

1 teaspoon Dijon mustard
1 teaspoon wholegrain mustard
1 teaspoon caster sugar

Make the mayonnaise, with the addition of the extra mustards and sugar. It is important that the mayonnaise is made before the grating of the celeriac as, if left on a board, the celariac will discolour very quickly. Putting the shreds in a bowl of acidulated water seems an unnecessary stage when it can go straight into the mayonnaise.

Take the celeriac and peel it, remembering that you do have to cut it quite deeply, as the gnarly skin is much thicker than on a lot of other roots. You want to carve away the slightly labyrinthine appearance of the inner skin. Cut the pieces to a size that will easily slide down a mandoline. When held to the light, the light should be noticeable through the slices – but they should not be paper-thin. If you have one, push through the appropriate setting on the mandoline to make batons. If using a knife, stack the slices up on each other, four at a time, and cut them thinly with a sharp knife, until all the celeriac is shredded.

Mix the celeriac through the mayonnaise and leave it to sit for a while, so that the celeriac tastes of mayo and the mayo tastes of celeriac. Do with it what you will.

PURÉE DE POMMES DE TERRE

I dare not say one word against the stalwart of the British table, mash, but sometimes I'd like one that is a little more luxurious and which will migrate a little further across my plate.

Serves 4

3 large Maris Piper potatoes, washed
large-flaked sea salt and black pepper

250ml single cream
50ml olive oil
3 garlic cloves, peeled

Preheat the oven to full blast.

Put the potatoes into the oven and cook for 1 hour until the skins are totally crisp. Take them from the oven in a tea towel and split them in half. Pick up each half, remembering you still need the tea towel and, using a fork, rake the white flesh out of the skins into a potato ricer and mash. I would not advocate using a processor, as this makes them very gluey.

In a pan, heat the single cream and olive oil together, along with the whole cloves of garlic. Bring the mixture up to a low simmer and keep it like this for about 10 minutes, until the garlic is totally soft. Do not boil the cream. Put the cream to one side.

When the potatoes are cooked and mashed, pour the garlic and cream mixture into the potatoes and stir until smooth and thoroughly mixed. Add some black pepper.

NOTE: *While writing this recipe, I was afraid to tell you (in case you thought it too much of a good thing) that when I was a trainee at the Halcyon Hotel this dish also contained butter. Go on, add a large fat knob to the cream and oil at the beginning.*

ROOT VEG CRISPS

I love cheap packet crisps, but here are some poncy ones. Root veg just squeak 'Me, me, me' from the soil or market barrow in autumn. These crisps remind me of piles of autumn leaves.

They are so easy to make. Cook them in individual groups, as they have different cooking times. If bagging them up, make sure they are totally cooled, or they will fade them like pets in a hot car.

Serves 1-6

6 large carrots
2 large beetroots
6 medium parsnips

$^1/_2$ celeriac
good vegetable oil, for deep-frying
5 cloves of garlic (optional)
20 sage leaves (optional)
large-flaked sea salt and black pepper

Peel all the veg (although with the carrots, beetroot and parsnips you retain the right to leave the skin on and personally I would). Wash the roots well.

Grate all the veg on a mandoline or adjustable slicer to a thickness of about 2mm. When held to the light, a crisp should be vaguely translucent. Grate the celeriac last, as if grated and left it will discolour.

Heat the oil to 180°C/350°F. Fry the crisps in batches, drowning them occasionally with the back of a slotted spoon and turning them. They will cook very quickly, in about 2 minutes if that. Be prepared to get them out fast. Strike like a kingfisher, as they will go on colouring even when lifted from the oil. Rush them to waiting kitchen towels, as you will need to go back to get the others out. Cook the beetroot last as it will discolour the oil. Fried garlic and sage leaves are a wonderful addition cooked in the same manner as the roots.

Allow them to cool before dusting over with salt and black pepper. I always eat crisps alone, as I can never hear what anyone is saying to me when eating them in company.

CORN ON THE COB

In our brief sweetcorn season, time is precious. I dedicate these fleeting weeks to leaving bite marks in as many stripped cobs as possible. Revealing the yellow corn beneath the husks is as enjoyable as unrobing a lover. Even butter slides across the corn with an apparent lingering. Every stage, from preparation to consumption, is a pleasure. If you buy corn, don't leave it around in the vegetable rack. Eat it immediately, as the sugars, when left, will turn to starch and, although still eatable, they will not give rise to a buttery smile. N.B. Tinned corn is for carp, why bother.

ELOTE TIERNOS (Sweetcorn with Mayonnaise, Cheese and Chilli)

The Mexicans really understand maize like no other nationality. Their country is its home. This recipe is one that you will find being sold on many streets across Mexico. I advise you to eat it with someone who thinks it's cute that you have blobs of mayonnaise about your face and bits of corn and cheese clinging to your jumper. This is not about manners. Be warned, though, there are no drop-in centres or maize workshops to help you through your subsequent addiction to this dish.

I prefer shop-brought mayo for this and Wensleydale seems the closest comparison to the crumbly cheeses used in Mexico. The bottom line is you can always use a mild Cheddar; a mature one would be a wrong turn.

Serves 4

4 corn cobs
4 tablespoons shop-bought mayonnaise
75g Wensleydale cheese, grated

1 lime
chipotle chilli powder or some
    pimentón de la Vera (hot smoked
    paprika)
large-flaked sea salt

Peel the corn cobs of their husks and threads. In a pot of boiling water with no salt, boil the corn for 8 minutes. While the corn boils, take two plates. On one dollop the mayonnaise, on the other grate the cheese. Cut the lime in half and have the chilli ready. If you have the chipotle chilli powder, great; otherwise, hot smoked paprika will get the job done.

When the cobs are ready, take them out of the water. Holding each one with a tea towel, drive a wooden skewer into the stem end. Now, holding by the skewer, roll them first in the mayonnaise thoroughly and then in the grated cheese. Sprinkle all about with the chilli powder or paprika. Finish with a little squeeze of lime juice and some salt. Relish not only the taste but also the mess you are creating.

CHESTNUTS

CHESTNUT SOUP

Shoulders hunched, arms crossed and stomping for cold, I cannot think of anything more warming than steaming ladlefuls of chestnut soup.

The chestnut itself immediately invokes pictures of glowing embers in the hearth, delivering comfort with every mouthful of its tan, sweet and generous meats. Very simple to make, this soup seems to throw a soft brown soothing cloak about the diner. The very idea of adding cream would be thoughtless, ignoring the natural creaminess the chestnut provides. If you are in possession of any young penny buns, once the soup has come to heat, they are excellent shaved raw over the top. It might sound pedantic, but I think this soup more appropriate for deep bowls than soup plates.

Serves 6

1kg fresh chestnuts (or 600g pre-prepared vacuum-packed)
25g butter
1 medium onion, peeled and finely diced
1 litre pheasant, chicken, ham or beef stock (*see* page 246)

soft brown sugar (optional, if using fresh chestnuts)
2 tablespoons Armagnac or other brandy
large-flaked sea salt and black pepper
good olive oil
a few cep or penny bun mushrooms (optional)

If you are using fresh chestnuts, use about a kilo, as, after accounting for peeling, rotters and the odd exploder, you will probably be left with the desired amount of meats. Those cooked in the fire, while viewing *Clash of the Titans* will require a little more attention than those roasted in the oven. They need to be turned and cooked as evenly as possible, avoiding any black burnt scabbing. The fire, however, imparts a pleasant smokiness to the soup.

The nuts must be cooked through and not have any bitey texture; the oven is effective for this. Put them in on full heat and cook them for about 20 minutes. Be wary on opening the oven door, as this can uncannily seem to prompt an explosion from within. (The chance of this can be lessened by a jab through the skin from the end of a sharp knife before roasting.) Hot chestnut shrapnel combined with alarm and surprise can be distressing. The pre-prepared vacuum-packed nuts are a simple alternative.

Take the nuts out and let them cool a little before peeling them, taking great care to remove the inner skin. This may involve breaking the chestnut to get into any creases. Try not to eat too many as you go.

Melt the butter in a saucepan and gently fry the onion until it is soft and dark golden. Remove from the pan and put to one side. Roughly chop the chestnuts and add them to the pan before pouring over the stock. Bring the pan's contents to a gentle simmer. With a stick blender or food processor, blend the soup until it is as smooth as possible. Pass the soup through a sieve if you have roasted the chestnuts from fresh, as this will remove any stray bits of furry skin or burnt flesh. Return the onions to the pan and pulse again.

Return the soup to the faintest simmer and cook it for **10** minutes. Add a little more stock if you think it too thick; it should be the consistency of floured gravy. Check the seasoning, and if you used fresh chestnuts you may want to sweeten them with a little sugar. Pour and stir in the brandy and cook for a further minute. Serve the soup, grating over slices of raw penny bun if you have them. Go over with a grind of black pepper. Finish with a good splash of quality olive oil. I have never been embraced by a bear, but I imagine it to be as warming as a bowl of chestnut soup.

BEETROOT

Many times I have drooped my head in despair for those who declare they don't like beetroot. Have you really tried it, I mean *really*? If you have only known beetroots as ping-pong-sized vinegar balls packed into wrinkly plastic and resembling surgical waste, then that is not what I mean. Or maybe it's the redness you do not like, as certainly I have come across a surprising number of people who have aversions to vegetables of a certain colour. But hope is at hand as beetroots also come in yellow and white.

I appreciate it is hard to escape horrors that appear in schools, pubs, and canteens but, cooked from fresh, beetroot is the most amazing vegetable. Properly heavy, swollen like a prosperous belly, and dense with their vivid sugary juices, they possess a texture like nothing else. Earthy and healthy, they exude a settling feeling. Once roasted they are fabulous vehicles for butter and salt and, if cooked further, they leak their sticky sugars and become delicious with crispy duckling. Simmered in a soup of ham, beef, cabbages and apples, or steamed and steeped in good olive oil, green herbs and anchovies, delightful. Once tasted you will be stained with joy.

When roasting or boiling beetroots, it is imperative that you do not peel them until they are cooked, as their taste, texture and colour will suffer.

BORSCHT (Beetroot Soup)

So often the English interpretation of borscht consists of little more than beetroot puréed in stock. There are thousands of variations from across Eastern Europe, but this recipe is the feast it can be; one to bolster hungry workers and tractor drivers, stir revolutionaries and tired writers while staining the shirts of greedy oligarchs. A statement in its blood colour alone, piping hot and full of essentials, this soup brims with vitality. Raise the red flag if serving borscht.

Serves 8

1kg beef shin or stewing steak
400g uncooked whole bacon, or smoked
    ham hock, or gammon
1 large onion
3 large celery sticks
4 garlic cloves
3 tablespoons vegetable oil
1 teaspoon dried dill seeds
2.5 litres water

a fistful of parsley stalks
3 bay leaves
4 large beetroots
2 Cox's apples
4 small parsnips
1 x 400g tin chopped peeled tomatoes
1x 400g tin white haricot beans
large-flaked sea salt and white pepper
50ml white wine vinegar
$^{1}/_{2}$ medium green or white cabbage
125ml soured cream

Preheat the oven to full blast.

Trim the meats. Peel and halve the onion and de-string the celery. Split the onion lengthways, dicing it all medium-fine. Slice the celery from tip to toe, reasonably thinly. Peel and chop the garlic coarsely.

Heat the vegetable oil in the bottom of a large lidded saucepan until just before it starts to smoke, and cast in the onion and celery plus the dill seeds, but not the garlic as you do not want it to burn. Stir around, really trying to get a bit of colour here and there. Now add the garlic. Turn the heat down, pour in the water and lower in the meats. Throw in the parsley stalks tied up with the bay leaves and bring everything to a gentle simmer. Put on the lid, adjusting the temperature, as the lid will increase simmering to boiling. You want to simmer this stock for about 2 hours. Check it a couple of times in the first 40 minutes, carefully skimming off any scum that rises to the top.

Meanwhile, de-stalk and de-whisker the beetroots, without skinning them. Give them a thorough wash before wrapping them up in foil. Put them in the preheated oven and roast them for the same time it takes the stock to come to greatness.

When the 2 hours are up, move the beetroots from the oven, tear open the foil. Take the meat from the broth and test; it should be deliciously tender. Remove it from the bones if using shin, and chop it into mouthfuls before returning it to the broth. If you like it, flop any marrow that might be hiding in the bones back into the broth.

Peel and coarsely dice the beetroots, putting them to one side. While keeping the broth on a low simmer, skin and core the apples, chopping them into small mouth-sized pieces, and do the same with the parsnips. Add them to the broth. Open the tin of tomatoes, drain away the juices and add along with the beans, also drained of their juice. Grind in a good amount of black pepper and season with a good measure of salt. Simmer the broth for a further 10 minutes with the lid off.

Add the beetroot and the vinegar before thinly slicing your cabbage and adding this too. When the cabbage is cooked, after about 10 minutes, the soup should be a rich, dark, rusty red. It is now ready to be served.

Make sure each person receives a good combination of meats, vegetables and broth. Have a large bowl of soured cream in the middle of the table to be spooned into each brimming bowl. Chopped parsley may be added here too. This soup is very nourishing and you can consume huge amounts without the feeling of overeating. Beware of making beetroot soup on Thursday, for it is said that the Devil will come to bathe in it, but maybe this was intended, as you scrub his back with a celery stick and do your deal.

LEFTOVERS: *Remember to save the beetroot tops. They are delicious wilted with a little butter in the same way as spinach, or added to salads and eaten raw.*

BEETROOT WITH GREEN SAUCE

A delicious way to enjoy beetroot, the preparation is very simple.

Serves 4

2 medium beetroots, stalks and leaves
    removed
olive oil
large-flaked sea salt

GREEN SAUCE
a handful of mixed fresh mint and parsley

2 level tablespoons baby capers
½ banana shallot, peeled and finely
    chopped
1 good hard garlic clove, peeled and
    finely chopped
6 tinned anchovy fillets in oil, drained
½ teaspoon Dijon mustard
4 tablespoons olive oil
juice of ½ lemon

Put the beetroots in a large pan, covered with water, and bring them to the boil. Simmer rapidly for 40 minutes, until tender, drain. Wearing rubber gloves, rub off the skins. Pick and finely chop the mint and parsley leaves, putting them in a bowl with the capers, shallot and garlic. Mince the anchovies before adding them to the bowl with the mustard. Add olive oil so it is just visible below the surface of the mixture. Everything slightly collapses, so don't add too much. Splash the lemon on sparingly. Mix and leave to stand. Chop each beetroot into eight and throw them steaming into a bowl before sprinkling a little salt about them and spotting them with the green sauce. Eat immediately as, left to stand, the beetroot will bleed into the sauce.

PEPPERS

RED PEPPERS WITH WALNUTS

Served in a pub raw beside a couple of grapes, some cress and a slice of orange, the red pepper is an unhappy sight, but roasted black and peeled, it is one of my favourite things. Combined with toasted walnuts and marjoram, I ate this in Fez in the presence of a fruity, heavily mascara-ed and rather ungainly belly dancer. Blushing to the same colour as the dish, it got more attention.

Serves 4-6

6 red peppers
a handful of shelled walnuts
juice of $^1/_2$ lemon

100ml good olive oil
$^1/_2$ cinnamon stick
large-flaked sea salt
a fistful of fresh marjoram or
    oregano leaves

Preheat the oven to full blast. Rest the peppers over a gas flame on a fork, charring the skins until soot black and blistered all over. This will take about 8-10 minutes for 1 large pepper. Alternatively, roast under a hot grill, turning regularly until the skin is blackened. Meanwhile, toast the nuts in the oven until dark golden, about 4 minutes. When cooled, rub them between the hands to remove some of the skin. Roughly chop and put in the serving bowl.

Allow the peppers to cool. Before skinning or deseeding them, nick each one near the pointed end with a knife and catch any juice from inside in a bowl. Rub and pull the skin off with your hands. Don't rinse the pepper under the tap, as the water will wash away the lovely charred flavour. If your fingers feel messy they, by all means, may be passed under the tap. Skin the peppers as well as possible. A few speckles of black do not matter though. Before de-seeding, tear the pepper lengthways into quarters. Holding each quarter the seeds can be shot into the bin with a directed flick of the wrist then, like a monkey picking over his companion, give them one final check for stray seeds. Alternatively, lay them flat and scrape out the seeds with a knife.

In a non-stick frying pan, briefly dry-fry the peppers on a high heat, to ensure they are entirely cooked. At the last minute add any juices you have collected, which will bubble and sizzle madly. Cook until they have nearly evaporated. They will add intensity to the peppers and why waste them?

Transfer to the bowl and mix with the walnuts. Squeeze over the lemon juice, pour over the olive oil and add the cinnamon stick, snapped in half. Season with salt, then allow to stand, covered, for an hour. Just before eating, stir. Roughly chop the marjoram or oregano and scatter over the top.

These peppers make a fine accompaniment to the lamb with bitter herbs on page 20.

POBLANO AND GOAT'S CHEESE

Although very much a mainstay of Mexican cookery, the poblano has taken well to English greenhouses, polytunnels and subsequently the kitchen. A dark blue-green, and slenderer than the green pepper, it can have an arresting heat, especially when allowed to ripen to red. When cooked, it is truly wonderful, imparting a very delicious buttery flavour.

Joy Michaud and her husband supply them from their company Peppers by Post (see below). Grown in a neat row of polytunnels but a 5-minute trot from the sea, the interior of each is like a mini rainforest. Being shown around one day, crouched beneath the humid foliage and surrounded by fat, dangling poblanos, Joy's love of chillies poured forth in one of the most fascinating 40 minutes I have spent with anyone. One thing that fascinated me is that, if you smoke, you must wash your hands before handling the chilli plants, as nicotine is poisonous to them.

Serves 4

5-6 large poblano chillies
200g sheep's curd or mild soft fresh
   goat's cheese

$^1/_2$ medium red onion, halved lengthways
large-flaked sea salt and black pepper
a squeeze of lime juice
50ml good olive oil
1 teaspoon dried oregano

Put the poblanos directly over the full flame of your gas ring and cook and peel them exactly as in the red pepper recipe on page 203. When they are done don't bother trying to capture any juice from within, as there will be none. Don't fry them either, as they eat best when *al dente* rather than cooked soft. Taking each piece, tear it into strips no wider than 2cm. Mexicans refer to these strips as '*rajas*'.

Crumble the goat's cheese or sheep's curd into the middle of your serving plate and arrange the *rajas* in, above and around the cheese. Peel the red onion half and slice it across in slivers as thinly as possible. Wash the slivers in a sieve under cold water to lessen the potency of the onion. Flicking off the water, scatter the onion over the cheese and *rajas*. Sprinkle all over with a little salt and grind of black pepper. Squeeze over the lime juice and pour over the olive oil. Lastly, really crushing it between thumb and forefinger, sprinkle over the dried oregano.

Together, the pepper's textural bite and faint heat combined with the tang of goat's cheese or sheep's curd and fragrant oregano is fantastic. I advise eating this unaccompanied by any other dish, with no interruption from other flavours.

NOTE: *Poblano chillies are available from a variety of sources including The South Devon Chilli Farm (www.southdevonchillifarm.co.uk; 01548 550782) and Peppers by Post (01308 897766; info@peppersbypost.biz).*

SWEET THINGS & BREAD

CHOCOLATE

CHOCOLATE TART

Done well, chocolate tart is a joy, but done badly, I'd rather eat a motorway Scotch egg. Recipes for it are often overly neurotic in their process, and I always approve of a good shortcut. So here is a brilliant one, based on Joyce Molyneux's, a chef I admire greatly. I have added coffee. This tart is foolproof – that is unless you are an utter nincompoop.

Serves as many as your mean slices allow

1 recipe sweet pastry (*see* page 248)
butter, for greasing
2 level tablespoons unsweetened cocoa
    powder

FILLING
600ml single cream
175g dark chocolate, 70% cocoa solids
1 tablespoon caster sugar
50ml strong or espresso coffee (optional)
2 medium eggs

Preheat the oven to 180°C/350°F/Gas 4. Grease a 30cm tart tin.
    Take your pastry from the fridge and roll it out between two sheets of greaseproof paper, flipping it over when needs be. Line the tart tin, chill and blind-bake as described on page 248. Allow it to cool. That was the hard bit. The rest is now laughably easy.
    Bring the cream to a simmer on a medium heat. In the meantime, break the chocolate into pieces and put in a food processor with the sugar. Add the coffee here too, if required. When the cream has come to heat, turn on the processor (the racket won't last long). Gently pour in the hot cream while the blades whiz round, then break in both the raw eggs. The hot cream will melt the chocolate. Whiz the whole lot for 20 seconds before pouring it straight into the awaiting tart case.
    Jiggle the sides a bit to help create an even surface and bring any air bubbles to the top. Leave in a cool place or the fridge to set. It will not take long. Don't go poking your fingers in it while it is setting; you will lose the velvet smooth surface and any self-respecting tracker will be able to follow your prints and hunt you down.
    Stand the tart at room temperature for an hour before serving. When ready to eat, sieve over the cocoa powder until you cannot see the filling underneath. Eat it!

ORANGES

CARAMEL ORANGES

This is such an effective and simple pudding, and a great way to finish a meal that might have been on the rich or heavy side, but watch out for the sharp if not dangerous shards of caramel once the top is smashed. When in season, the winter blood orange makes a striking replacement, or, if combined with any of the more common varieties, a very pretty dish indeed.

Serves 6

8 large oranges or 12 blood oranges

150g caster sugar
water

Peel the rind from four of the oranges with a potato peeler, then slice the rind into long strands no wider than a matchstick. Cover with water, add a tablespoon of the sugar, and simmer until soft. Drain and keep the rind to one side.

With each of the eight oranges, slice off the bottom, sitting it flat on the board. From the top, using a sharp knife, cut away the rind and pith, fully exposing the fruit underneath. Turn the orange on its side and slice it into ¼cm-width rounds, putting them in the serving bowl. Remove the pips as you find them. Mix in the rind.

Pour the remaining sugar into the bottom of a saucepan – I would advise a non-stick one. The pan must be totally clean, as any pieces of unknown detritus will stop the caramelizing process. Cover the sugar with water and bring it to a gentle boil. Continue boiling gently for about 15-20 minutes, after which you will notice the sugar beginning to change colour. Some areas of the pan will seem to colour faster than others, so very gently swirl the sugar syrup in order to keep a universal colour throughout. I like my caramel to go quite dark, but without taking on the bitter burnt taste that spells too far. This colouring stage should be guarded very closely, as the slightest wavering of attention might necessitate starting again.

When the caramel is to your liking, pour it about the oranges in a thin stream, where it will spit, settle and finally set hard. Leave the oranges to stand for at least half an hour, letting some of the caramel melt into the orange juice, the rest remaining crisp on top. How simple can a pudding be?

I'm learning that some people hate combining fruit and chocolate puds. As one who does not agree, these oranges go well with the chocolate tart on page 210 or, more simply, with an excessive splash of double cream.

APPLES & PEARS

An apple to fruit is like water to drinks; reliable, always there. Pick up a good one and that same voice comes back, 'I seem to have forgotten you. I must eat more apples.' You stare at it, see the white-faced bite mark and think, 'wow this is good'. I have no idea how an Indian reflects on an Alfonso mango, but there is something so English in our apple's juices, so reassuring when felt clenched in the hand and polished like a cricket ball. It is the apple snatched from the branch and scrunched, or brought from the barrow and then tossed in the air to land back in the hand, that puts a spring in my step. Apples remind me of drowsy wasps, packed lunches, the pleasant smell of fermenting sweet rot, brown cores found under the car seat, penknives and cheese and old knotted trees, so easy to climb. So raise your pint of cider to those old orchards that have seen so many changes beneath their branches.

BAKED APPLES

This is a pudding of abundance, like a bountiful pirate's chest crammed with goodies. The Bramley is great for it, its tartness counteracted by the goodies.

Serves 4

5 tablespoons shelled walnuts or hazelnuts
8 fresh Medjool dates, roughly chopped
2 tablespoons good dark runny honey
1 level teaspoon ground cinnamon
a good pinch of ground cloves
a good grating of nutmeg
4 heaped tablespoons white breadcrumbs

4 tablespoons currants
2 tablespoons candied peel
4 medium Bramley apples

BRANDY BUTTER
100g butter
4 tablespoons dark muscovado sugar
3 tablespoons brandy, or to taste

Preheat the oven to **200°C/400°F/Gas 6**. For the brandy butter, bring the butter to room temperature. Cream it in a bowl until pale. Beat in the sugar gradually, then add the brandy, a dribble at a time, so that it does not split.

Toast the walnuts in the oven until coloured, about 5 minutes. Put them, chopped, in a bowl with the dates, honey and spices. Toast the breadcrumbs in the oven until golden and stir them into the stuffing with the currants and peel. Core out each apple with a 5cm hollow. Cut into the skin in two parallel lines in a band across the middle. Cut out a square of greaseproof paper wider than the apple and put it on a baking tray. Put the apple on the paper. Pack the stuffing into the hollow and put a big dollop of brandy butter on top. Bake in the preheated oven for 40 minutes, until soft without burning.

APPLE CHARLOTTE WITH STEM GINGER

A molten hot volcano of appleyness, Charlotte really is a winning pudding and an excellent way of using a glut of apples that might be left lying around in the grass. I am a huge fan of ginger, but by all means leave it out if you are not, or replace it with something else – although I would not recommend cola cubes.

Serves 4

6 Cox, Braeburn or Russet apples
4 knobs of stem ginger in syrup, with
    3 tablespoons syrup

juice of $^1/_2$ lemon
125g butter
$^1/_2$ white farmhouse bloomer loaf
    (avoid a sliced bagged white)
1 small jar or carton clotted cream

Preheat the oven to its maximum.

Peel and core the apples, and chop them coarsely. Put them in a pan with the ginger syrup, lemon juice and 3 tablespoons water. Simmer them gently until they are totally soft, about 20 minutes. Purée the apple mixture with a blender stick until it is the texture of baby food – if it is too runny, it can always be reduced a little. (I would note here that texture will be given by the chopped ginger.) When the apple is cooked, chop the ginger into medium dice or thin slivers. Try and choose a ginger that's really poky, as I don't see the point if it has no heat.

Put the butter in a small pan and gently simmer to clarify it, skimming off the curds as they rise to the top. I find this process strangely mesmeric, waiting for the little white islands to rise up through the golden pool. When properly clear, put this to one side. A little residue on the bottom of the pan isn't a problem.

Cut the crusts off the loaf, reserving them for your feathered friends outside or to use as breadcrumbs in another recipe. Slice the bread carefully. Use a cold loaf as shop-warm it will rip. Cut it to the width of the nail on your little finger.

Using a 16cm pudding basin, rest the basin on one of the slices and cut around the base, creating a circle for the bottom. Taking the clarified butter and a pastry brush, paint the bread circle on both sides and place it in the bottom of the basin. Cutting the other bread slices in half, brush them with butter on both sides and place them around the inside of the basin, making sure they all overlap by about 1cm. This is important as, while cooking, the hot apple magma will find any exit it can and spoil the crisp armoured exterior.

When inserting the last piece of bread, make sure that it both overlaps and goes under the first piece. You should still have a couple of slices of bread remaining for the roof of the Charlotte. When buttering the pieces, don't be mean: really daub the pieces properly.

Fill the bread casing with the apple sauce. Fashion a roof with the remaining butter-painted bread. Cut two circles of cardboard to fit the inside of the top of the basin and wrap together in foil. Put this on top of the basin and weight it down with weights such as cleaned stones. Put in the preheated oven and cook for about half an hour. Check after this time – it will be very obvious whether the bread is cooked, as you will see any colouring on the edges very clearly. This colour will be the same throughout the rest of the bread and you want it to be a good dark gold. The top, though, will be less cooked, as a result of its being covered. So remove the weights and foil lid and return the Charlotte to the oven for a further 7 minutes. It will not achieve the same colouring as the outside, but don't worry about this, as it sits unseen on the bottom, and will not ruin the look.

When ready to eat, up-end a plate on the top of the basin and invert the basin on to the plate, using a tea towel or oven cloth so as not to burn your hands. Take away the bowl.

When back at the table, dramatically smash in the top of this molten apple volcano and spoon in two large dollops of clotted cream, which will disappear into the hot apple interior. Attack with spoons, being careful not to immediately blister your lip with your first mouthful.

POACHED PEARS

Although cooking an unripe pear will make it soft, I suggest you start off with one that is ripe and tasty to begin with. Any variety will do. The pear must be soft with a silky syrup to coat your throat with spicy sweetness. A good pear is so simple to achieve and I would far prefer to eat a tinned pear than any home-poached bullet that shoots into your lap when a spoonful is attempted.

Serves 6

6 pears
4 tablespoons caster sugar
1 bottle red wine
125ml brandy

AROMATICS
1 orange and 1 lemon

1 thumb-sized knob of fresh root ginger
1 teaspoon freshly grated nutmeg
6 cloves
3 bay leaves
1 cinnamon stick
1 teaspoon fennel seeds

Peel the pears and stand them in a pot in which the wine can rise up to the stalks. Scatter the sugar all over them and pour in the wine and brandy. I would advocate using good ingredients, but the wine in this case need not be top quality (a cheap Côtes du Rhône is fine). The same applies to the brandy.

Put the orange and lemon in the sink and pour over boiling water to remove any wax. With a potato peeler, remove half the rind from both fruits in nice long strips. Pop this in the pan with the pears. Squeeze in the juice of both. Skin your ginger and slice it into very fine rounds so you can eat it (as I do not see the point of cooking something edible only to ignore it). Add the ginger to the pan, along with all the other aromatics.

Bring the contents of the pan to a slow simmer and poach the pears for half an hour. The pears should not be bitey, but properly cooked through. This is easily discovered by resting the blade of a sharp knife on one of the pears – it should slide in easily. Taking them off the heat, gently remove them with a slotted spoon, while remembering that any roughness with the spoon will cut into the pear, ruining its looks. Leave to one side to cool.

Return the juices to the heat and cook to the consistency of cough mixture. A thin syrup does not cling and will make the dish look watery.

Pour the syrup into an airtight container and lie the pears in it. Try not to snap off the stalks when handling the pears; I think they look better on. Leave the pears for about a day, turning them two or three times, so that they take on a dark colouring on all sides.

Serve them cold, with a slice of the chocolate tart on page 210, or with those old favourites, shortbread and cream.

BLACKBERRIES

After scratching and bloodying throughout the year, the bramble offers up its autumn truce with its juicy blackberries. Like a kingfisher on minnows, one must strike fast and snare the treats before the harvesting force of old ladies robs the hedgerows blind. (An open receptacle is best when picking, as a bag will result in an inadvertent smoothie.)

Foxes love blackberries too and, either in juicy ecstasy or simply marking their territory, will wee on the bushes. The same goes for dogs. So pluck the higher fruit. I'd steer clear of even the juiciest blackberries from busy roads unless you like to scrape monoxide conserve across your toast in the morning.

BLACKBERRY ETON MESS

This is not strictly Eton Mess, the original being made with strawberries. What I love about this dish is its chaotic appearance, not unlike my own. The reason why this recipe makes 12 meringues while only using six is to leave you with a few extra to munch messily over your computer while working. Once tested, this really only serves one.

Serves 6

500g blackberries
40g caster sugar
juice of ½ lemon

50ml cold water
284ml carton double cream

MERINGUES
4 large egg whites
225g caster sugar

Preheat the oven to 150°C/300°F/Gas 2, and line a large baking sheet with baking paper.

For the meringues, whisk the egg whites in a large bowl using electric beaters or a hand whisk until they form soft peaks. They are whisked enough when you can turn the bowl upside down without them sliding out.

Next, add the sugar, a tablespoon at a time, whisking well between each addition until it is all incorporated. The meringue should look really thick and glossy at this point, like a handful of gentleman's shaving foam. Drop 12 large spoonfuls of the meringue on to the baking sheet, spacing well apart. Place in the oven, reduce the temperature to 130°C/250°F/Gas ½ and bake for 1¾ hours until the meringues are crisp. Turn off the oven and leave them to cool with the door shut.

To make the blackberry purée, place 200g of the blackberries in a

small pan with the caster sugar, lemon juice and cold water. Bring to the boil, then reduce the heat and leave to simmer gently for about **10** minutes until they are very soft, stirring occasionally. Remove from the heat and purée using a stick blender until smooth. Leave to cool.

To assemble the Eton Mess, very softly whip the cream until it is just holding its own. Roughly break six of the meringues into a large bowl; avoid the temptation of crushing them tightly in one hand like a movie thug powdering a snooker ball in his fist. You want the pieces to be quite large, not dust. Add the cream and blackberries. Fold loosely together using a large spoon, adding the blackberry sauce over the top. Don't over-mix before finally adding one last scribble of sauce. I'm not including any suggestions for leftovers here, as I would be very surprised if there were any.

SLOE GIN AND BLACKBERRY JELLY

As I rarely eat jelly, I would happily have my tonsils put back in order that I could have them taken out again to give me an extra excuse to eat this.

Serves 6

4 gelatine leaves
600g blackberries

400ml water
4 tablespoons caster sugar
juice of 1/2 lemon
150ml sloe gin (*see* page 244)

About half an hour before doing anything else, break the gelatine and soak it in just enough warm water to cover. In the bottom of a pan place the blackberries with the water, sugar and lemon juice. Bring to a gentle simmer, and cook until the fruit has totally collapsed and fallen apart.

Place a sieve lined with a double layer of muslin over a bowl and drain the blackberry mixture until every drip of juice has been extracted. Don't press the pulp, as this will make for a cloudy jelly. Discard the fruit pulp.

Reheat the fruit juice gently, to little more than warm, and whisk in the gelatine, really making sure you eradicate all lumps. Take the liquid from the heat and pour in the sloe gin. Pour it into your **700**ml jelly mould, and leave overnight in the fridge with a plate over the open end. Rabbit shape is my favourite.

When ready to serve, fill a large saucepan with tap-hot water to just under the level of the jelly in its mould. Place the mould in this water, and count to no more than **20** seconds. Put a plate over the top of the mould, remove from the water and up-end. Hopefully, you will hear a faint sucking sound as the jelly releases from the sides. Lift the mould off carefully. Behold, your wibbly-wobbly creation.

I think few things are better than single cream poured all over the top.

PLUMS

PLUM COMPOTE

Flopped into the middle of hot porridge or plain yoghurt, poached plums start most of my early autumn weekdays. I loved them out of a tin at school and love them now pulled from the tree, the juice dripping from my chin, savouring that slight crunch of a lazy wasp that failed to vacate an unobserved hole. The most famous plum I ever ate belonged to Pink Floyd's Roger Waters, snatched off a branch overhanging his neighbour's field where I was fishing. Sadly, its taste was not as remarkable as hoped.

Serves 4

8 large, ripe plums
freshly squeezed juice of 1 orange or lemon

100g caster sugar
approximately 850ml water

Make a shallow cut all the way around the middle of each plum with a sharp knife. Put them into a medium saucepan – they should fit fairly snugly. Add the orange juice and sprinkle with the caster sugar.

Pour over enough cold water to just cover the plums (but don't use too big a saucepan). Bring the contents up to heat and then simmer gently for approximately 10-12 minutes. The plums should be tender but not breaking apart. Remove them with a slotted spoon and place them in a serving bowl.

Return the pan to the hob and boil hard for a further 15 minutes or so, until the sauce is well reduced to a syrup that is slightly runnier than cough mixture. Pour it over the plums and leave it to cool. Have fun spitting the stones into a paper bin from a distance, moving the bin a little further away every time.

LEFTOVERS: *Make a Plum Cooler by adding fizzy water, a twist of orange rind and ice to the plum syrup and mixing it in a highball glass. White wine can be a very good replacement for the fizzy water, effectively making a spritzer with plum syrup.*

QUINCE AND PLUM CRUMBLE

When at school, the continual taunts of 'Fat Val' were water off a duck's back when left with my spoon and crumble.

Serves 6

butter, for greasing
6 quinces
160g caster sugar
6 large ripe plums
juice of $^1/_2$ lemon

CRUMBLE
175g plain flour, sifted
50g caster sugar
50g dark muscovado sugar
100g butter, cold and cut in small chunks
100g porridge oats
finely grated zest of 2 lemons and juice of $^1/_2$

Preheat the oven to 160°C/325°F/Gas 3. Butter an ovenproof dish of about 30cm square.

Put the quinces in an oven tray, and scatter most of the sugar around them. Add 200ml water, cover with foil, and put them into the preheated oven for about 3 hours, where they will take on a dark colour, getting redder and redder the longer they are cooked. Check after 2 hours to see that they still have water in the bottom of the tray. Splash another 100ml of water about the fruit. When ready, remove the foil and allow them to cool. Peel the quinces carefully, and slice off all the flesh, wasting none.

Wash and chop the plums, removing the stones. Combine all the fruits and juices together, adding the lemon juice. Put this in the bottom of your buttered crumble dish, scattered about with 1 more tablespoon sugar.

In a bowl, while the quinces are cooking, rub together the flour, sugars and cold butter chunks. It is important that the butter is cold, or you will end up making more of a dough than a crumble. When a crumbly feel has been achieved, throw in the oats and lemon zest. Combine these well and put the crumble mix in the fridge until needed.

When all the fruits are awaiting, scatter the crumble mix across the top. Do not dry it out with too much crumble mix. Cook the pudding in the oven for about 45 minutes, or until it is a dark golden, nutty colour. Serve it with lashings of good, vanilla-y custard.

NUTS

BAKEWELL PUDDING

If you asked me my view of Bakewell Tart, my answer would once have been 'take it or leave it'. I've been missing out, though, for having tasted it one weekend at a friend's house, I now love it and regret all those times I could have eaten more. After some tinkering at home, here is my version. It's pretty good, although not as yellow. But, shock horror, I think this dish cannot be called a Bakewell Tart, only a Bakewell Pudding, as I've been told that to qualify as a tart it must be made in the town of its name. I would prefer not be kidnapped by the Bakewell People's Front, to be tarred in hot jam and feathered with flaked almonds while I'm jeered at in the High Street.

Makes 1 tart

1 x 30cm blind-baked pastry case, made with Bakewell pastry (*see* pages 248/9)

FILLING
200g raspberry jam
1 fresh vanilla pod or 1 teaspoon vanilla extract

300g butter
300g caster sugar
200g ground almonds
100g plain flour
1 teaspoon baking powder
3 medium eggs, beaten
3 tablespoons flaked almonds

Preheat the oven to 150°C/300°F/Gas 2. Spread the jam across the bottom of the cooked pastry case. If using, scrape out the vanilla seeds from the split pod.

In a food processor, blend together the butter and sugar until creamed. Next, add the ground almonds, flour, baking powder, eggs and vanilla seeds or extract (put the emptied pod into your vanilla sugar or save it, wrapped and stored in clingfilm, for making custard). Blend well.

Spoon the almond mixture on top of the jam and spread it evenly around the inside of the cooked pastry case. Bake in the preheated oven for half an hour. Scatter over the flaked almonds and return it to the oven for another 20 minutes.

I would suggest covering your large warm slice of tart with cream, as employed here it works better than custard. The tart, whoops pudding, eats well cold.

MONTE BIANCO

This treat is not as heavy as it may sound and is definitely one of my favourite puddings. I would use pre-packed and peeled sweet chestnuts.

In its look it should at least imitate its namesake in miniature. However, lacking in piping bag skills, mine resembles no mighty mountain capped with snow, but rather an odd heap. Therefore, I think it better for me to suggest that the whipped cream is actually a large cloudbank gathering over the Alps.

Serves 4

450ml whole milk
500g pre-cooked vacuum-packed chestnuts
100g caster sugar plus 3 tablespoons

1 tablespoon unsweetened cocoa powder, plus 1 teaspoon
3 tablespoons brandy or grappa
150ml whipping cream
100g caster sugar

In a pan, bring to a simmer the milk, into which you have dropped the chestnuts, and gently cook them together for approximately 10 minutes. Transfer the milk and chestnuts to a food processor and purée until smooth. While the contents whiz around, add 3 tablespoons caster sugar, the teaspoon of unsweetened cocoa powder and the brandy or grappa (the latter 1 tablespoon at a time). Turn out the mixture and allow it to cool. Cover the surface with loose clingfilm to prevent a skin from forming.

Spoon the chestnut mixture into a piping bag or strong plastic bag with the corner cut off. On to a plate, pipe your chestnut purée through a nozzle or hole that squeezes the mixture to about earthworm size. Going round and round in a scribble pattern, squeeze all the mixture into a large cone shape. You must fill the middle too, or the mound will collapse. This airy spaghetti resemblance makes the pudding taste quite light.

Cover the 100g caster sugar with water in a clean pan. Put it on to boil and get the caramel going. In the meantime, the mountain now needs toning. Sift the remaining cocoa powder through a fine sieve over the top. You will see that it creates a darkness where it falls, leaving any underside pale.

Get the caramel quite dark, but not bitter. Swirl it occasionally during the darkening process as this will ensure it does not burn in one place but colours evenly. When the caramel is ready, gently pour it thinly around the peak of Monte Bianco, where it will cascade down the slopes, setting as it goes into streams of crunchy caramel. You do not need to use it all.

Lastly, add the icing sugar to the cream and beat together until it can just hold its own shape. Don't whip it too stiff, as it's not nice to eat. Fashion it about the mountain top to give an impression of a cloud or snow. Serve immediately while trying to get more of the caramel than anyone else. This is a wonderful dish.

BANANAS

BAKED BANANAS WITH RUM

I have decided to include an unseasonal recipe, but because for me bananas are such a big part of eating during the mean months, I just thought, what the hell. This is my mum's version.

Serves 6

6 bananas, peeled, cut in half and split
    lengthways
50g butter
2 good tablespoons dark muscovado sugar
freshly grated nutmeg
125ml dark rum

juice of $1/2$ large lemon or 1 large lime

TO SERVE
1 x 280g shop-bought gingerbread loaf
a knob of butter
1 tablespoon runny honey
double cream

Preheat the oven to **200°C/400°F/Gas 6**.

Place the bananas in the base of a heavy ovenproof dish. Dot the butter about evenly, a bit on the bananas, a bit on the bottom of the dish. Sprinkle over the sugar and grate some nutmeg hither and thither. Splash over the rum, and squeeze over the lemon or lime juice.

Put the dish in the preheated oven and cook for about half an hour until all the contents are bubbling and sticky. After **10** minutes, put your loaf of gingerbread in a dish in the oven, also dotted about with butter and honey.

Take everything out together, and serve the bananas with slices of the gingerbread and some cream.

BREAD

CHILLI CORN BREAD

Piping hot home-made cornbread revealed from a tea towel is a fantastic accompaniment to meats and beans from my barbecue. Filling, with that unmistakable corny taste, it also goes with bacon, pushed around the frying pan to mop up the excess fat. It's real basic eating, a bread that I can never imagine slicing, but one that should be broken up in big crumbly chunks and eaten following the cry of 'Come and get it!'

Serves 4–6

75g butter
1 plump red chilli, deseeded and finely
    diced
200g maize flour
150g self-raising flour
1 heaped teaspoon baking powder

$1^1/_2$ teaspoons large-flaked sea salt
black pepper
2 corn cobs, husks removed
2 large free-range egg, separated
150g buttermilk
150ml whole milk
25-40g mature Cheddar cheese, finely
    grated

Preheat the oven to 190°C/375°F/Gas 5.

Melt the butter in a small, ovenproof frying pan on the hob. Add the chilli and fry gently for 1-2 minutes, until softened, stirring occasionally. Remove the pan from the heat and set aside.

Mix the flours, baking powder, salt and a couple of grinds of black pepper in a large bowl. Holding each corn cob upright on a chopping board, cut down the length carefully with a small, sharp knife to remove the kernels. Scoop the kernels into the flour mixture and toss everything together. Make a well in the centre.

In a bowl, whisk the eggs lightly with the buttermilk and milk. Stir quickly into the corn mixture with a large metal spoon, but don't over-mix. Next, stir in the melted butter and chilli to form a cake-like batter. Add a little extra milk if your batter seems too thick. Flop the mixture into the warm frying pan.

Level the surface with the back of the spoon and sprinkle with the Cheddar cheese. Bake in the preheated oven for about half an hour, until well risen and golden brown. Serve warm in generous wedges.

IRISH SODA BREAD

Tom Halifax is a very nice man who lives on a tiny magic island protected by guard otters and some particularly ferocious cattle. He makes delicious bread and, as I have always avoided baking, I thought I'd better pay attention. You have to get close to see the process, as his wee house is filled with dense peat smoke from the fire. How easy he made it look and how delicious this bread was. Using no yeast, it is less bloating than other breads, although this is not the case if you immediately finish a loaf when hot from the oven all slavered with a packet of butter and pot of jam. Tom advises you make two loaves for exactly this reason.

Makes 1 loaf

250g plain white flour, not strong flour,
   plus a few extra handfuls

250g wholemeal flour
1 teaspoon large-flaked sea salt
1 teaspoon bicarbonate of soda
450ml buttermilk

Preheat the oven to 200°C/400°F/Gas 6.

Sift the white flour into a large bowl and mix in the wholemeal flour, salt and bicarbonate with a whisk to lighten it. Make a well in the middle and add most of the buttermilk. Mix with a metal spoon. You need to use your judgement at this stage. What you want is a sticky but not liquid dough. If it is too dry and crumbly, add a little more milk; if on the other hand it is too wet, scatter in a little extra white flour. Most importantly of all, this mixture needs to be well combined. If in doubt, err on the side of wetness, as a dry loaf will fall apart.

When done, flour your hands and lift the dough on to a well-floured surface. When you have made a fairly even lump, lift the dough into the middle of a floured tray and flatten it into a disk about 5cm thick. Scatter more white flour over the top of the dough and cut across the loaf both ways to make a cross, about halfway through.

Put the bread in the preheated oven for about half an hour. We like a really crusty top, so give it an extra 5-10 minutes if necessary.

Cool it on a wire rack so that that it does not go soggy underneath. You can break the loaf in quarters (or 'farls') along the cuts. Make sure that you taste some of the loaf with butter when new and hot. The loaf will keep well, the texture becoming firmer, after a day or so. There is no better bread for toast I know of. It also makes great croûtons for soup.

SIX DRINKS
& BASICS

MEAT TEAS

As a medicinal restorative or a steadier, meat tea is always a welcoming bolster for a cold or out in the cold. When you feel wobbly like a new foal or more seriously hung over, collapsed like an ancient mule in the market and being whipped by your brutish owner, then no preparation could be less taxing than simply heating up some good stock and dressing it appropriately. With the addition of a small nip from the hip-flask, I have also found it to limber up the swing when I'm shooting like a clot, or to clear the head when snivelling under the oppression of a piggish cold. Here are two versions: one for early autumn and one for mid-winter.

HOT CHICKEN TEA WITH MINT AND LEMON

Serves as few or as many as you like

good chicken stock (*see* page 246)

fresh garden mint
lemon
freshly ground black pepper

Gently heat the required amount of stock on a low simmer. While it heats, put a small sprig of mint in a glass or cup with a slice of lemon. Before pouring the stock into the receptacle, add a good coarse grind of pepper and an additional small squeeze of lemon juice. Pour on to the lemon slice and mint, and don't burn your lip. A shot of vodka can be a happy addition to this tea.

HOT BEEF TEA WITH CHILLI SHERRY

Makes about 1.5 litres

1kg shin end of beef
4 celery sticks
2 small onions, unpeeled
2 leeks
4 carrots
any mushroom skins you happen
   to have saved
a splash of vegetable oil
1 teaspoon English mustard powder

3 litres water
3 bay leaves
6 black peppercorns
freshly grated nutmeg
a splash of red wine vinegar
a splash of Worcestershire sauce
1 teaspoon tomato purée
chilli sherry (*see* page 243)

TO FINISH
4 medium egg whites and their shells

Choose a stew pan large enough to be able to properly stir the ingredients in the initial stages so they do not tumble out on to the floor and get kicked

under the washing machine. Cut the meat into big fat chunks. After washing all the vegetables thoroughly (do not bother to skin them), chop them in a similar fashion to the beef.

Heat the vegetable oil in a pan until it is smoking and then cast in the meat with the mustard powder, stirring it all around from time to time. When the meat begins to colour, chuck in the vegetables and fry for a further 5 minutes. When you notice dark 'catchings' sticking to the bottom of the pan, add the water and all the other ingredients except the whites and shells. When the broth achieves a low simmer, set the gas and cook uncovered for $1^1/_2$ hours. At first you will notice a scum rising to the surface. Skim this off.

When the time is up, strain the liquid slowly through a fine sieve into a clean saucepan. (Do not throw away the contents of pot one, as herein lies a meal – *see* leftovers below) Bring the stock or tea back to a very low simmer, just quivering. Blitz the egg whites and shells in a blender and stir it all into the broth. The egg white mixture will immediately rise to the top and form a crust, which will filter out any remaining murk in the tea. After 6 minutes, turn off the heat and carefully remove the egg white layer with a slotted spoon. Pass the tea through a sieve lined with a muslin cloth, aiding it through with the caress of a spoon, gently scraping the bottom of the sieve.

Cool the tea, cover, and then store it in the fridge. When taking beef tea into the field, simply heat it up and transfer it to a vacuum flask. Take the chilli sherry (*see* opposite) with you. Pour the tea into the cup and sneak in the sherry where appropriate. Making beef tea is well worth the effort, as it really is an excellent hot drink.

LEFTOVERS: *Fork out the beef, which will be very tender, with any of the poached veg that you fancy. Arrange them on a plate, scattering over a small handful of baby capers and a little chopped fresh parsley, and eat with a good dollop of **Dijon** mustard. If you want to eat it later, simply heat up what you have kept with a little splash of water before adding the accompaniments.*

ALCOHOLIC DRINKS

COURTFIELD CHILLI SHERRY

I encountered this fiery alternative when staying with friends in Herefordshire. I have their permission to pass it on.

1 bottle medium sherry or manzanilla
a small handful of bird's eye chillies

6 black peppercorns

Create some room in the bottle for the additives by immediately taking a large swig from the top, or pouring yourself a glass. Add the bits and bobs, replace the top and store the sherry for at least a week, before which you will not experience the full pokiness.

SPICED CIDER

This drink is truly fantastic for warming the bones and getting any party started, although with my lot that's hardly difficult.

Serves 6

1 big knob (double thumb size) of fresh
    root ginger
1 big sprig of fresh thyme

300ml good apple juice
2 heaped tablespoons muscovado sugar
2 cinnamon sticks
1 litre bottle good medium dry cider
6 measures of Armagnac or other brandy

Peel and finely slice the ginger, throwing it into the bottom of a large saucepan. Add the thyme, apple juice, sugar and cinnamon sticks. Pour over the cider and Armagnac or other brandy to taste, and put the whole potion on the hob, getting it very hot but on no account simmering or boiling it, which would destroy the alcohol content. Ration it out with a ladle into glasses, although after an hour rationing is pointless.

SLOE GIN

This is my father's sloe gin recipe and will be too sweet for some tastes, but I'm writing it exactly as it was. He measured everything visually by pints, using a measuring jug for both liquids and solids and not embracing the metric system. He normally used 3 pints' worth of each of the ingredients, for a house normally well stocked with half-wine bottles filled up with this drink. This recipe makes enough to get you through the winter.

1 pint sloes
1 pint caster sugar
1 pint gin

Raid the hedges blind, incorporating bullaces with sloes if they should be growing together. The bullace is almost exactly the same as the sloe, but larger in size. On returning home, and having consumed large amounts of buttered toast and jam, set about the berries with a sewing needle, pricking each one.

In our family, all the ingredients were then put into a large stone flagon that could receive everything used. So, into a sterilized, airtight, large-necked preserving bottle, poke all the pricked berries, pour the sugar, and glug the gin through a funnel. The flagon was then corked and left under the dining-room table, where it was positively encouraged that three times a week guests push it around with their feet while eating lunch or dinner. This below-table process used to go on until Christmas, the sloes having been picked in October.

After this period of time has passed, take the small armoury of empty half-wine bottles you have saved and put a funnel, lined with some washed jam muslin, in the top of one. Decant the sloe liquor into the bottle. Repeat and cork them all, making sure you date them so that, if you want to, you can note the differences between the vintages. They should now be put down until the following Christmas, although the longer you leave them the better. Enjoy with mince pies, or from a small flask when out in the field. I do not advise getting drunk on sloe gin, as the aftermath is unbelievably painful.

Howard, the photographer of this book, has suggested making sloe gin with no sugar in it at all, saying it is remarkable. Although I haven't yet tried this, many of the other things he has brought to my attention I have enjoyed thoroughly.

SLOE GUN

The following drink is a variation on the French 75, a delicious cocktail named after a famous field gun. I have replaced the gin with sloe gin.

Serves 1

40ml sloe gin (*see* opposite)
3 ice cubes

a squeeze of lemon
Champagne, to top up
a twist of lemon rind

Into a slender straight glass, pour the sloe gin over the ice, adding the lemon juice, Champagne and finally the twist of lemon rind. I would recommend no more than two before dinner.

STOCK

GOOD CHICKEN STOCK

This uses the wreckage of the Sunday chicken. Continue as follows.

When making this stock, the more bones you add, the more intense it will be. Don't include the lemon you may have roasted with your bird, as it will make your stock bitter and distasteful. Pull away excess fat before making your stock; although it has flavour, discarding it will not lessen the stock's deliciousness and will prevent it from becoming greasy if boiled at too high a temperature. The slower you cook your stock, the clearer it will be. Peelings may be kept for stock, and although adding them will give a rounded flavour, use what you have if veggies are scarce.

Makes about 1.2 litres

a fresh free-range chicken carcass (roasted on a high heat for 20-30 minutes until well browned) or the bones and leftover meat from a fresh roasted chicken
2.5 litres water
2 medium onions, peeled and quartered
2 celery sticks, cut into short lengths

1 leek, trimmed, cleaned and cut into short lengths
3 medium carrots, trimmed and cut into short lengths
4 garlic cloves, unpeeled
2 bay leaves
4-5 sprigs of fresh thyme
parsley stalks, if to hand

Place the bones in a large saucepan with all the remaining ingredients. Bring to the boil. Skim any scum from the surface as it rises, and as soon as the water begins to boil, reduce the heat to very low and cook, uncovered, for 2-3 hours. The water should gently burble during this time – any more frantic activity and the heat should be reduced further.

When ready, remove from the heat and strain through a colander into a large bowl. Leave the bones and vegetables sitting over the bowl until they stop dripping – but don't press, as this could result in a cloudy stock. Next, tip the liquid through a fine sieve (lined with muslin if you like) into a large container. Leave to cool and chill, covered. Remove any fat that rises to the surface before using (this is easier to do if it is set in the fridge). It will become gelatinous and should be used within 3 days or frozen for up to 3 months.

GOOD BEEF STOCK

Cutting away excess fat will help you achieve a clearer stock. If you don't have any gnawed beef bones handy, buy some from the butcher and roast them in a hot oven at 200°C/400°F/Gas 6 for about half an hour, turning twice. Drain before using and pat dry with kitchen paper. Or *see* Meat Teas on page 240, and skip the egg stage, depending on how clear you like your soup.

Makes about 1 litre

3 tablespoons sunflower oil
3 medium carrots, trimmed, halved
    lengthways and cut into short lengths
2 medium onions, unpeeled and quartered
2 leeks, trimmed, cleaned and cut into
    5cm lengths

3 celery sticks, cut into 5cm lengths
mushroom peelings, if to hand
6 garlic cloves, unpeeled
2 tablespoons tomato purée
1.5kg roasted beef bones (left over from
    a roast rib of beef)
approximately 3.5 litres water
3-4 sprigs of fresh thyme
2 bay leaves

Heat the oil in large frying pan over a medium heat and fry the carrots over a high heat until beginning to brown, turning regularly. Add the quartered onions, the leeks and the celery, plus the mushroom peelings if using, and fry until the vegetables are golden brown all over. This will add flavour and colour and will take around 12-15 minutes. Stir in the garlic and tomato purée and cook for a couple of minutes, stirring constantly.

Place the bones in a very large saucepan and cover with the cold water. Put over a high heat and, when the water comes to the boil, skim any scum from the surface. Tip the vegetables into the pan and stir in the herbs.

Return the pan to the boil and, as soon as it reaches boiling point, skim any scum from the surface and reduce the heat to very low. Simmer gently, uncovered, for 4-5 hours, skimming occasionally. The water should gently burble during this time – any more frantic activity and the heat should be reduced further.

When ready, remove from the heat and strain the liquid through a colander into a large bowl. Leave the bones sitting over the bowl until they stop dripping – but don't press, as this could result in a cloudy stock.

Next, tip the liquid through a sieve lined with muslin into a clean pan. Return to the hob and boil hard until reduced to about 1 litre.

Leave to cool and chill in a covered container. Remove any fat that rises to the surface before using (this is easier to do if the stock has set in the fridge). The stock should become gelatinous and should be used within 3 days or frozen for up to 3 months.

PASTRY FOR TARTS

All the recipes for tarts in this book require blind-baking, as I have politely eaten too many soggy-bottomed tarts, the ruination of often fabulous fillings. So, when using pastry, here are a few things you knead to know.

First, all the recipes in this book are measured to fill an 11-inch (27.5cm) tart tin with a removable base. I use a non-stick one, as it releases the pastry case with ease, thus lessening the chance of damaging the tart.

Roll out the pastry to the thickness of no more than a one-pound coin. Make sure that the pastry can be easily lifted from the work surface, helped by a fine dusting of flour, which you should also apply to the rolling pin.

After it has been made, the pastry must rest. If chilled and rolled out in a warm kitchen, by the time it is ready to be lifted to the tin, it will be limp and impossible to work with. Cold pastry, although harder to manipulate, allows you time. I'd suggest a minimum of 1 hour in the fridge once made.

When putting your pastry in the tin, make sure the sides reach right into the corners. Otherwise, a pocket of air will be created which, when heated, will blow the case's edges out, creating sloped sides.

The pastry must be weighted down or it will rise up. Line your pastry case with a sheet of baking paper, pour in a good amount of ceramic beans and spread them out evenly: a generous amount is essential to stabilize the sides. Always use baking paper rather than foil, as foil can stick to the pastry, and, when peeled away, may break it.

If warm pastry is put straight into the oven, it will shrink quickly, whereas pastry that has been rolled out and rested in the fridge its tin will not. Therefore, if you plan to trim off the excess before baking the tart, please rest it in the fridge before baking. Alternatively, if you leave the sides hanging over, this will prevent the edges shrinking below the line of the tart case. The excess can then be trimmed away by gently rubbing the blade of a knife around the top of the tin.

ROUGH PUFF PASTRY

Makes around 1kg (2 Venison Pies and 6 Bill's Onion or 2 Autumn Pastels)

450g plain flour

a good pinch of large-flaked sea salt
375g cold butter, cut into 2cm pieces
250ml cold water
1 tablespoon lemon juice

Ideally make this pastry the day before so it has time to chill. Sift the flour and salt into a large bowl and drop in the butter. Toss it around with a large metal spoon to coat it in flour. Mix the water and lemon juice and pour it into the flour and butter. Use a round-tipped knife to cut across the bowl several times, turning it continually while chopping the butter into the flour until the dough comes together. When it forms a loose lump, tip it onto a board and quickly shape it into a fat slab, roughly the dimensions of a brick. Flour the work surface well and roll it out to a rectangle approximately 38x20cm.

Fold one-third of the dough to the centre, then fold the other third over that. Roll it into the same size rectangle you started with. Fold in exactly the same way again. Rotate the pastry in a quarter turn. Continue rolling, folding, pressing and turning a quarter-turn three to four more times. Don't worry too much if the butter makes its way through occasionally in the early stages, just keep the board and pin well floured.

After the last folding stage, wrap the slab in clingfilm and chill for several hours. If it's very firm, let it warm for a few minutes before rolling. Divide it in half as you won't necessarily need it all in one go. It freezes well.

SHORTCRUST PASTRY

FOR SAVOURY PASTRY:
Makes enough for 1 tart case
340g plain flour
200g fridge-cold butter, chopped
2 egg yolks
a dash of water

FOR SWEET PASTRY:
Makes enough for 1 tart case
350g plain flour
50g caster sugar
200g fridge-cold butter, chopped
2 egg yolks

FOR BAKEWELL TART PASTRY:
Makes enough for 1 tart case
275g plain flour
80g ground almonds (add with the flour and sugar)
75g caster sugar
225g fridge-cold butter, chopped
3 egg yolks

Put the flour in a food processor (add sugar at this stage too if making sweet pastry) and blitz in with the butter. When the mixture is in fine crumbs, start adding the egg yolks, which you have beaten – this stops them streaking the pastry (this does not apply to Bakewell) and water. When all is combined, bring it together with your hands on the work surface, but do not knead it. Wrap it in clingfilm and rest it for 2 hours in the fridge. Preheat the oven to 190°C/375°F/ Gas 5. Roll out the pastry and fill the cases, filling them with baking beans as described opposite. Cook them for 20-25 minutes before removing the beans and paper and returning them to the oven for 5 minutes until nicely rich and golden in colour.

RAZ EL HANOUT

I become the secret spice grinder when mixing this magic combination, hunched over my measurements like a smith tinkering with gunpowder.

For the purposes of availability it is important to realize that there are many variations on this recipe. I live in a Moroccan area of London and have talked on the subject of raz with many locals. Some versions from the kitchens of great palaces are said to contain up to 60 obscure spices, powders, barks and seeds, but on the whole they are much simpler, most with little more than the seven essentials: cumin, cinnamon, saffron, cloves, turmeric, coriander seeds and salt. Use what you have, and here is mine.

Makes 100-150g

20 dried rosebuds
1 tablespoon dried lavender
5 dried bay leaves
1 cinnamon stick
1 teaspoon ground star anise or 3 whole stars
2 teaspoons ground galangal

1 teaspoon each of ground cloves, allspice, good saffron strands, cayenne pepper and freshly ground black pepper
$1/2$ whole nutmeg, freshly grated
12 cardamom pods, seeds kept and husks discarded
1 tablespoon fennel seeds
1 tablespoon coriander seeds
1 tablespoon black mustard seeds
1 tablespoon cumin seeds

Put all the flowers, bay leaves, cinnamon stick, star anise and ground spices into a blender or coffee grinder, but do not press go. Place all the seeds in a frying pan and place on top of a medium heat. Pay attention to them, stirring them and making sure they do not smoke or burn. When the coriander and mustard seeds begin to pop, add all the seeds to the blender or coffee grinder and blitz until you have the finest powder possible.

Your magic powder is now ready. Take a smell and realize the alchemy you have created, like the mad wizards of the desert. 'With this formula all power will be mine, mwah-ha-ha-ha-haaaaaaa...'

Highly recommended with chicken, guinea fowl, lamb, all game birds and as yet untried by me on fish.

LEFTOVERS: *When preparing coffee, raz can be a delightful addition. Maybe not for the morning cup, but preferable at about three in the afternoon. Just put 1 full teaspoon in a cafetière with the ground coffee and pour it out as normal. Good black or white.*

A POTTED HISTORY

Melting plastic soldiers on light bulbs or heaving rocks into the slurry pit were some of the childhood pastimes I approached with gusto. Deconstructing the world was hungry work, leaving my brother and me like greedy eagle chicks that gulped down everything. Animal fats, mangosteens, chicory, jugged hare and other early indulgences normally saved for adulthood: we were born with inquisitive young stomachs and stout little hearts.

Both parents were exceptional cooks. My mother approached the stove with quiet flair and an ability to deliver endless crowd-pleasers and inventive new creations, such as warm curried crab custards and glasses containing tinted aspic, suspending quail's eggs and tarragon leaves. My father on the other hand was most operatic, bearing down on every pan, spoon and sieve, a lot of alcohol and flames and the exclamation, 'Never enough sauce!'

With food so utterly delicious, the table was a competitive arena. Dinner companions would suddenly lose their footing, mid-conversation, as distracted Warner eyes patrolled the table concerned that guests, or God forbid family, were taking too much. My brother's knowing little wink as he pronged an extra chop would render me speechless, my napkin throttled under the table.

When I wasn't fighting him for the tattered remnants of a Helmut Newton's book of nudes, I would bury myself in my mother's collection of cookbooks, avidly reading the recipes of Elizabeth David or staring at sun-faded pictures of casseroles on loose Carrier recipe cards. The information was digested and logged, but the cake was yet to rise.

I've been fortunate to delight in soufflés that floated from the plate towards the heavens, but also encouraged to eat striped snails picked from a hot Greek wall and baked with wild spinach. This, coupled with adventurous holidays, instilled in me an early understanding that dishes from humble origins (tinned goods, I salute you) often delivered equal satisfaction to those of extravagance. Meals prepared by an old grandmother hunched like a croissant or grilled lake fishes from a petrol station are, in fact, the tastes that remain closest to my heart. These memories, alongside a love of nature, formulated early notions of environment brought to the plate; those things that work together and those that do not. A grouse will never step beneath the shade of a coconut palm.

Born fidgety, nervous greed grew into the constant search for more good food and tasty treats, the joy of taste leading to endless larder skirmishes. Co-ed schooling delivered sparse snogging, so I turned my attention to the local fish farm and school nature reserve. Rods and air rifles, buried in the grounds, were employed in rampant poaching. Prolific quantities of trout, rabbits, blewits, parasols and the odd pheasant were raced

back, under a jumper, to the out-of-bounds sixth-form kitchens, where my housemaster turned a blind eye in exchange for the occasional potted rabbit or cured trout, an alternative to conventional sponge accomplishment from home economics.

School led to art college in London, and I moved into a tiny bed-sit above a sawmill off the city's Holloway Road. It was here that I really started playing with food. Once back in my tiny room, the window would be thrown open, the film of wood dust wiped away and my loyal four-ringed Belling put to good use. By the time I left, I think few North London bed-sits had served up such an array of dishes: goat with camomile and bitter herbs, stuffed cabbages and experiments with octopuses. My fellow tenants said they would miss the cooking smells on the stairs.

Soon after leaving college, I decided to put down the brush and pick up the spoon. I spent five years under London's dining rooms where my practices were whipped into shape. Since then, I have sent thousands of morsels towards thousands of mouths, occasionally investigating other career diversions, but I've never stopped cooking at home. A treasured constant, a consuming meditation, my cure for restlessness, it is in the kitchen that everything outside it can wait. Whether to satisfy a particular hunger, test my own computing after eating elsewhere, or act upon a hunch, it is in this deeply personal space that food is prepared for those with whom I choose to share it. Purchases and inspirations, notes from trips, or the appearance of ingredients I have long ignored give me an urgency to return home to my favourite room.

Sitting back as the steam swirls up and others lean in to help themselves, I'm filled with the warmest glow. Resting on a walk, pasty in hand, a pickled egg in the pub, drying mushrooms in a cupboard, poaching chicken for a terrible cold or breaking into reluctant sea urchins while seated upon a rock: food is so often the embodiment of the place it is eaten in. Me, well I'm here to eat, born to cook and forced to work.

INDEX

ACKNOWLEDGEMENTS

Love and duck fat to…

Mitchell Beazley what a great company. It's been a real pleasure.
   Becca Spry, you are the bees knees and beyond the phone call of duty. I can't thank you enough.
   Susan Fleming, one of the coolest women I have ever met. With good coffee, bad typing, the kitchen scales and the occasional rolled eye, we got there.
   Howard Sooley, for his excellent photos. The only dude I've ever worried could potentially out eat me.
   Justine Pattison and Steve Parle, the most calming people to cook with, who both have an unnatural ability to survive my chaos and make the unlikely possible.
   Caz Hildebrand, your layout is ace and you're soothing like warm cocoa.
   Tim Foster, for letting me go something like 'I prefer this one, no actually can I change it for that one… would it be possible… actually errr'.
   Diana Henry, you're great you are.
   Tony, Ed 'nice plums' Cain and Alan, the three marketers. Thanks for the top stuff, but earlier next time, huh.
   Elizabeth Sheinkman, for handling the things that make me nervous.
   Hattie Ellis, for her wise words.

Everyone at Optomen, especially my *sensei* Paul 'you know what I mean' Ratcliffe, Gary, Ian and Faye. Pat and Ben, you know what I think. Richard 'the hobbit' Hill, Derek the Mexican and Rex.

Every supplier who delivered the things I knew or now know they are so good at.
   All the contributors I will meet and learn from in the series, who I had not yet met when writing this.
   All the chefs and cooks I learnt from, especially Alastair Little, although you might not know it.
   My tiny kitchen, who I love dearly.
   And of course my friends. My fridge is your fridge.